GAMLINGAY

six hundred years of life in an English village

James Brown

CASSELL

'For Joseph'

First published in the UK 1989 by
Cassell Publishers Ltd,
Artillery House, Artillery Row
London SW1P 1RT

Copyright © James Brown 1989

First published 1989

Distributed in the United States by
Sterling Publishing Co, Inc.
2 Park Avenue, New York, NY 10016

Distributed in Australia by
Capricorn Link (Australia) Pty Ltd
PO Box 665, Lane Cove, NSW 2066

British Library Cataloguing in Publication Data

Brown, James
  Gamlingay: 600 years of life in an English village
  1. Cambridgeshire. Gamlingay. Social life, history
  I. Title
  942.6'57

ISBN 0304 316288

Printed and bound in Great Britain by Mackays of Chatham, PLC

Contents

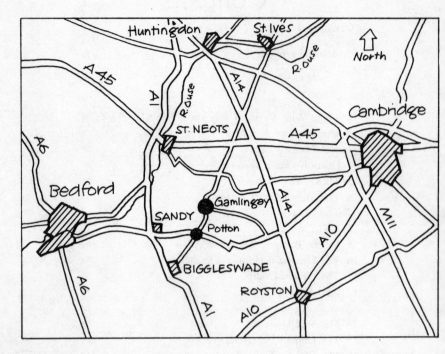

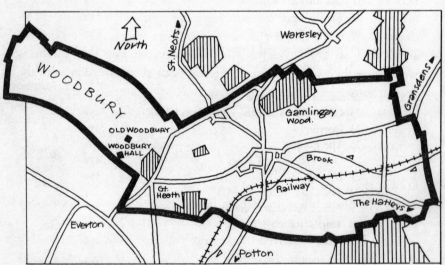

⬡ Woodland.

Sketch maps of Gamlingay parish and surrounding area. The ancient parish was the largest in West Cambridgeshire, comprising 4,460 acres and stretching some five miles from east to west. Woodbury was transferred to Bedfordshire in 1965.

Foreword

It will be a sad day for England, and for that unique institution the English Village, if the time ever comes when village histories cease to be written and read – however badly written some of them may have been in the past and will continue to be, no doubt. For a village can inspire loyalty in a way few other entities can, and we are nearly all of us villagers in origin if we trace our roots deep enough in time. We are all what we are, character-wise, mostly because our rural forebears were what they were. However pressing our preoccupation with the present, however desperate our concern for the future, we do have an interest in the past; why else would we persist in boring the younger generation so often with our reminiscences?

Moreover, history is nowhere so completely epitomised as in the village. You cannot tread one yard of village soil that has not known the tread of human feet for more than a thousand years. An egg is not more full of meat than is an English village full of history – the difference being that there is no such thing as bad history.

It has been said – indeed I have said it myself – that the history of one village is in a sense the history of them all. There are 13,418 places mentioned in the Domesday Books; somebody must have counted them. So allowing for deserted medieval villages, villages created during the Middle Ages, villages which became towns (they were all once called towns) and so on, there must be some twelve thousand. Of course, they don't all have the same history, but they all had manors, lords, serfs, villeins, courts, commons, paupers, pestilence, free-thinkers and fornication, etc. Therein they are all alike, or nearly so.

In other ways the villages differed sufficiently – as regards geography, for instance – for that difference to affect materially the course of each village's history. Jim Brown believes that the Gamlingay story was profoundly influenced by its geographical location, and he could well be right. Villages also differed in that there were places which, from their very beginnings, often for reasons no one can any longer explain, were 'mean' places, troublesome spots, places where one could expect to encounter more than the average run of 'wrong 'uns' – more sinners than saints. Again, Gamlingay seems to have been one of those, if the impression I have formed from this book is correct. Such villages were common enough; I can think of half a dozen I know. However, the distinction between 'sinner' and 'saint' was never one of the easiest to make. In which category, for instance, would one place John Bunyan? Anyway, a preponderance of sinners tended to enhance a village's interest, even in the eyes of its neighbours. There's still some satisfaction to be had from uttering the remark: '. . . people are a rotten lot', the blank being filled by the name of the next village, or next but one.

For the village historian, however, the most significant difference is the varying extent to which documentary evidence relating to his village has survived in legible form, and is available. For some villages it is almost negligible; their history can never be written. For a surprising number of villages, however – probably a majority – the material is very considerable (in some cases amazingly so) and often its extent is not yet realised or exploited. Until all the documents have been catalogued, until all the muniment chests of the Cambridge University Library, the Bodleian, the British Library, the Public Record Office, the colleges of Oxford and Cambridge, the County Archives, Diocesan Records, etc., have been exhaustively searched, let no one say that there is nothing more to be known about the history of a particular village.

In respect of source material, Jim Brown has been outstandingly fortunate, commendably diligent and truly wise. Lucky enough to discover a really fantastic amount of documentation – one series alone involved some seven hundred photocopies – he has combed and sifted it to ensure that no illuminating scrap was overlooked, and then put something like ninety per cent of it to one side. The worst fault he could have committed would have been to try to use it all. I have tried to read village histories whose authors (no names) have done just that. There is no surer way to bore readers to flight, or sleep. For a good ninety per cent of the entries in village documents *are* boring. The writer needs them for the drop of knowledge they impart; but the reader does not.

Having said that, I must hasten to say that there are no rules controlling the writing of local history. For that matter, there are no rules for controlling the writing of national or international history apart from what political bias or religious prejudice counsels. There are, however, in my view, three criteria which the local historian ought to observe if he can – even if he insists that he is not writing 'history' but a 'story'.

He (or she) should only write what he knows to be true or has strong reason to believe to be true, based on the evidence. He does not have to 'prove' it by cluttering up his text with numbers referring to notes giving references to sources – though he may say where he got the information, if he thinks it necessary. And he can, indeed must, admit the possibility of an error of interpretation.

He (or she) ought to try to write only what is of interest to the reader. This is not quite the gamble it might seem. There is one topic which can safely be counted on to interest most people, and that is – people. Lots of village records consist simply of lists of people, plus sums of money or numbers of family or servants or windows or dogs. That is not very interesting. Many more records concern people's misdemeanours, strife, passions, strivings, and these *are* interesting. If a writer should stumble upon a juicy scandal embellished with picturesque detail, then he is on to a certain winner.

Finally, the resulting book, assuming one has reached the point of going into print – and by no means all village historians do, mercifully perhaps – must have readability, whatever else it lacks. Many readers will even pardon the neglect of the other two criteria if the story is eminently readable.

How does Jim Brown's *Gamlingay* measure up to my standards?

Admirably. He passes the test with flying colours. He has written the truth in an interesting manner, and produced a *very* readable book with which I am proud to be associated.

Rowland Parker
Cottage on the Green
Foxton
Cambridge

Acknowledgements

One of the many pleasant discoveries I made during the fourteen years it took to research and write this book was the unfailing courtesy and help I received from the staff of the various record offices, libraries and archive repositories I consulted. I am grateful to them all, particularly the staff of the Public Record Office, the British Library, and the Bodleian Library in Oxford. I am especially indebted to Mr J.M. Farrar, the County Archivist, and his staff at the County Record Office in Cambridge. They kept me supplied with an almost endless stream of photocopies over a period of several years, and promptly and politely provided me with every document I wanted to see during my visits to them. Similarly, the help I received from Mrs D.M. Owen and Dr E.S. Leedham-Green, Keeper and Assistant Keeper respectively of the Archives in the University Library in Cambridge, was invaluable. I must also express my gratitude to Mr M.J. Petty and his staff at the Cambridgeshire Collection in the Central Library in Cambridge for their assistance. Likewise I owe a large debt to Dr J.R.L. Highfield, the Librarian and archivist of Merton College, who went to extraordinary lengths to obtain copies of the College records for me.

Grateful acknowledgements are also due to the Warden and Fellows of Merton College, Oxford, the Reverend Tydeman, the Syndics of the University Library, Cambridge, the County Record Office, Cambridge, and Canon Longford for permission to quote from the records in their keeping.

I must also thank the many friends who helped during the gestation of this book, particularly Alec Marshall, Paul Housden, Anne Dibbs, Rex Whitfield, Angela North, Alan Hibbitt, Peter Froste and Doug Titmus. David McGregor and Jim Dew very kindly loaned me their family documents and one splendid map at a time when I was desperate for exactly the information they contained. My old friend Geoff Wilkie not only read the book in draft form and made many useful suggestions, but also pushed and prodded me to write it in the first place. Jenni Brown was always understanding about my need to write. Debbie Prime gave me the peace of mind and encouragement I needed to rewrite the book for the umpteenth time. She and Jane Moore also read the book and made many helpful comments, as well as showing great faith in my limited abilities.

My own family took an interest in the book. I picked my father's brains about an assortment of subjects relating to Gamlingay and my mother read the book in draft.

Lastly, I must record my everlasting debt to the late Rowland Parker, from whose friendship and example I learned so much. He encouraged me, read and criticised my work, and argued with my conclusions. He prevented me from making a fool of myself on several occasions, and pointed me in the right direction on numerous others. By taking a fatherly interest in an enthusiastic amateur he taught me to approach a fascinating subject in a new way. He has my deep and sincere thanks.

Introduction

This book tells the story of the ordinary people who lived in the village of Gamlingay, and, through them, of the village itself. They, like the village, were by and large unremarkable. The only thing that makes them seem different to us is the fact they they lived in a world that has vanished. Were we to live in their world I am pretty sure we would act exactly as they did. Strip away our layers of accumulated knowledge and our veneer of civilisation, and underneath we are the same.

The book covers the period from 1279 to 1850. This is because before 1279 documentary evidence from Gamlingay about the rural world of open-field, communal village agriculture is rather sketchy. After 1279 this is no longer the case. Rather, the opposite is true. The year 1850 is significant because it marks the end of that way of life with the coming of enclosure. Put another way, my story starts at the zenith of medieval open-field farming and ends with the painful death-throes of that system some six hundred years later.

Gamlingay lies at the western edge of Cambridgeshire, close to both the Bedfordshire and Huntingdonshire borders. It is and always was the largest village in west Cambridgeshire. It also happens to be the village in which I spent my childhood. I grew up among the fields and streets and many of the buildings which appear in this book. I was christened in the same font as most of the people you are about to meet. The village was part of me. I saw it in its summer glory and its winter coat of snow. I saw the harvest gathered each year, and the green explosion as the woods, fields and hedgerows burst into life with the coming of spring. And all the time as I was growing up the village was telling me something of its past. I only dimly perceived this at the time, of course. Nor did I realise that the village was also asking me questions. Later, when I had moved away, those questions came back to me again and again. Attempting to answer some of them I became interested in its history, as most people are interested in the history of their village.

I began a little idle research. I soon discovered that by sheer accident a flood of documentation has survived from the medieval and later periods (Gamlingay must be one of the best-documented villages in England). Idle research became complete immersion. What those dusty, frustrating, sometimes impossible documents eventually told me became the basis of this book.

But I am not a historian, and what I have written is not history. It is a true story, based on historical evidence. As such it contains no footnotes or references. I hope that anyone who wishes to use the original documents I have used will be able to find them from the list of documentary sources at the end of the book. Most of the story is based on primary sources, but occasionally where the evidence is missing or vague I have had to speculate. Where I have speculated I have made it clear that that is what I am doing. My speculations are based on historical probability and have reference to the facts. If there are any errors in the book (with so much translation and transcription it could not be otherwise) I apologise for them and wish to make it clear they are the fault of nobody but myself.

For much of the period covered by this book the calender year began officially on 25 March. Wherever possible I have changed those dates affected into modern ones. On the other hand I have made every effort to retain the original spellings used in the documents, partly because it would be difficult to decide on a standard form for many words, particularly field-names and surnames, but also because to modernise them would be to rob the documents of much of their charm, although I have used capital letters where I thought it would make them easier to understand. Likewise, punctuation is virtually non-existent in the original documents. I have added it.

The maps of the village and its surrounding fields on page xvi will give you some idea of what Gamlingay was like in 1279. It was a compact village, most of the houses facing the Cambridge to Bedford road, each one standing in its own long, narrow piece of land. It had its church, its village green, and two manors, both sited beside the brook. There was a third manor within the parish but outside the main village: the manor of Woodbury, lying a mile or so to the west. In its essentials the village of 1279 was little altered from its Saxon predecessor of three or four hundred years before. It was to remain recognisably the same village for the succeeding 600 years.

Like the rest of the Midlands and most of East Anglia the parish fields were farmed on the 'open-field' system, or by 'champion husbandry' as it was also called. For arable purposes the land was split into three large fields, known sensibly enough as East, Middle and South, with each one lying fallow in strict yearly rotation (a glance at the map of the parish on page xvi will help you locate them). This was the only reliable method then known of returning fertility to the soil. The other two fields not lying fallow were cropped, one with winter-sown corn, mainly barley, and the other with spring-sown corn, beans, peas and so on. This method of revolving land use – tilth, breach, fallow – would continue, although there was to be a move towards more compact holdings, and a little Tudor enclosure, to disrupt the endless cycle. Within these huge, unhedged fields each man's holding was divided into long thin strips scattered among the furlongs (smaller, more manageable units) which in turn made up the great open fields. In this way a man's land was spread out all over the parish. Despite the obvious drawbacks of this unsophisticated system it did ensure everyone a fair share of both good and bad land. It also meant that everyone holding land within a particular field or furlong was forced to grow the same crop as his neighbours. The field of winter-sown corn, for instance, could hardly contain anything else.

Growing the same crop as everyone else meant that the enterprising peasant could not experiment with new techniques for producing better crops, nor try out new varieties. Yields, too, were often desperately low. In a good year the villagers could produce enough food to feed themselves, but in bad years they starved. The conservatism of rural life – doing something the way it had always been done – precluded any real progress in agriculture until the seventeenth and eighteenth centuries.

The Hundred Rolls of 1279 are the first documents to tell us in detail about the medieval village. They were compiled in an attempt to discover, parish by parish, who owned the land and, more importantly, by what right they held it. The Hundred Rolls survive for only six English counties, but the surviving portions have been printed and are available in most County Record Offices, although still in their original abbreviated Latin form. Luckily the Cambridgeshire Rolls are among the survivors, so we will begin with them.

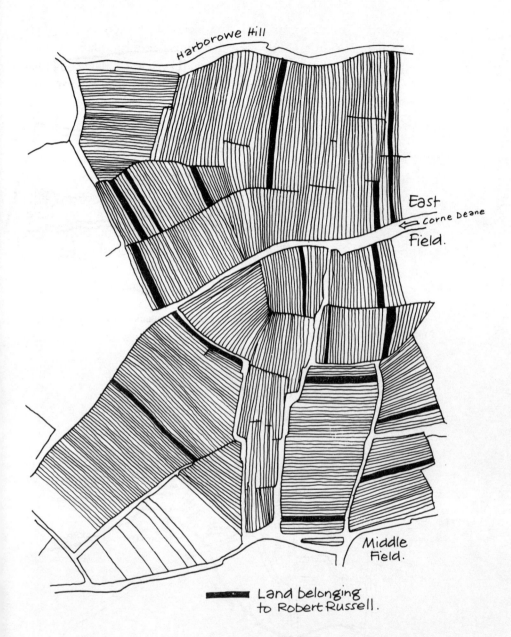

Harborowe Hill

East Field.

← Corne Deane

Middle Field.

▬▬▬ Land belonging to Robert Russell.

This sketch map of part of the East field is taken from Langdon's maps of 1602. For the sake of clarity I have not included all the strips shown by Langdon. The strips in black show how the $8\frac{1}{4}$ acres belonging to Robert Russell in this part of the parish were distributed. Land was held like this from the Middle Ages until Enclosure.

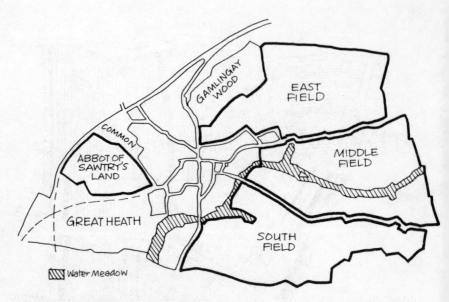

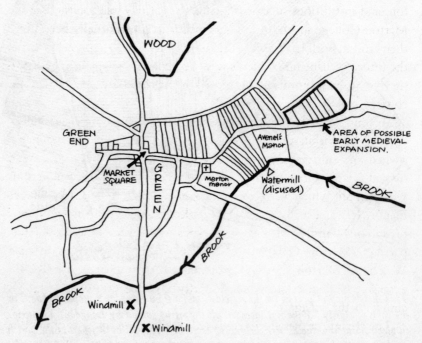

The village fields in 1279. The three great open fields remained virtually unchanged until the middle of the nineteenth century.

The village in 1279.

1

Those Who Mattered and Those Who Did Not

In 1279 Gamlingay was unequally divided between the few who owned the land and the many who did not. The landowners were known as 'lords': men like Sir John Avenel and Sir Hugh de Babington; and institutions such as the Church, various religious houses and Merton College in Oxford. These institutions had usually been given their land in both large and small amounts by people anxious to secure the future well-being of their souls. The charters recording these gifts survive in vast numbers in record repositories up and down the country.

Sir John Avenel and Merton College owned the two long-established manors within the village itself, while Sir Hugh de Babington owned the outlying manor of Woodbury. The Abbot of Sawtry owned a large block of land which became more important as time went on, but which was never quite large enough to be a fully-fledged manor. It was usually leased to a single tenant. The Avenels were a prosperous family who owned estates in several Cambridgeshire parishes. Merton College acquired its manor through its founder Walter de Merton shortly after 1260, when it became part of the extensive College estates. Indeed, Merton College still owns a sizeable chunk of the village today.

The tenants of these lords consisted of villeins of one sort or another and 'freemen', who, as their name suggests, were not subject to the rigid rules governing the lives of the villeins. If you were born a villein you stayed a villein. In the legal parlance of the time you owned 'nothing but your belly'. A villein belonged to his lord. He was a chattel, bound hand and foot to the manorial soil, and could be sold along with the rest of his lord's estate. Although there were shades of meaning within the all-embracing term 'villein', each with a different name, they were all variations on the theme of bondage.

Free tenants could, and frequently did, hold land from more than one lord, as well as indulging in a tangle of subletting among themselves. In 1279 most of the land owned by Sir John Avenel, Merton College and Sir Hugh de Babington was leased to free tenants. Sir John Avenel leased about 270 acres to forty-three free tenants, another forty-three held about 350 acres from Merton College and nineteen held around 115 acres from Sir Hugh de Babington.

Of the unfree tenants the customary tenants, so called because they did work ('services') for their lord based on custom as well as paying rent, held on average between six and ten acres each, barely enough to scrape a living from. Avenel had eleven customary tenants holding 120 acres or so, and there were eight on the Woodbury estate holding around sixty-five acres, but there were none on Merton manor. The cottars, named after the 'cots' (cottages) they held, had no land and survived as best they could, grazing a cow on the commons if they could afford one and hiring themselves out when not required to work for their lord. Again, Merton had no cottars, but Avenel had nine, paying between 6d. and 2s. a year for their cottages, and there were also nine on Woodbury manor, paying between 1s. and 3s. 3d. for theirs. The fact that only thirty-seven tenants were unfree probably has more to do with the historical fact that Gamlingay had been (just) a part of pre-Conquest Danelaw, well known for its preponderance of free peasantry, than to any generosity on the part of its overlords.

The services owed by the unfree to their lords are given in detail in the Hundred Rolls. I shall quote just one. In return for a house and six acres of land Geoffrey le Ster, a customary tenant, owed Sir John Avenel 'every week of the year two work-days whenever he must, and a day at weeding, mowing and lifting hay' as well as three 'boon-works' during the harvest. Furthermore he was to be reeve at the lord's wish, was not to allow his daughter to marry without licence, must give his 'best beast in lawful heriot' when he died, and owed an arbitrary tax called tallage to his lord at Michaelmas 'as the lord wishes'. If this seems like exploitation to us it probably seemed all the more so to Geoffrey le Ster and the rest of the unfree. In fairness, these services were not always exacted in full, and even if they were there was often a grown-up son living at home who could act as a stand-in. Usually, too, a day's ploughing or carting ended in the early afternoon when the tired oxen were put out to grass for the rest of the day, while a day-work is thought to have ended around noon.

Exploitation, though, as the Hundred Rolls make abundantly clear, was not simply a matter of working for one's lord. Apart from being a continual reminder of his bondage the practical reason why a villein was not allowed to marry his daughter to another lord's man without licence was that the lord could charge him for the privilege. This charge was called 'merchet'. In fact much of the villeins' energy was spent in finding the means to pay for 'privileges' like this. He had to pay tallage each Michaelmas *at the lord's will*, come what may. He had to pay to leave the manor, pay if his son wished to leave the manor, pay to inherit his holding, pay for not inheriting it, pay to grind his corn at the lord's mill and pay if he was caught not doing so. Even when he died he had not finished paying, or rather his family had not, since they were forced to hand over his best beast in 'heriot'. And when he had finished forking out to his lord there was always the

Church. Tithes, often as bitterly resented in the Middle Ages as they were in the nineteenth century, took an annual tenth of a villein's income, while his second-best beast, assuming he had one, was taken as 'mortuary' in lieu of tithes it was assumed he had neglected to pay in his lifetime. Then there were mass pennies and church scot, fine-sounding names for taxes claimed from time to time by the Church, not to mention those taxes levied by royal command.

There were two avenues of escape from this manorial oppression open to the discontented villein. He could up and leave in the middle of the night for the nearest town and if he could remain there uncaptured for a year and a day he was deemed to be a free man. His lord had four days in which to recapture him and bring him back to the manor, using force if necessary. After four days the lord had to resort to the law to get his recalcitrant chattel back: a typically medieval mixture of common sense and absurd legal convention. It was a double-edged sword as far as the villein was concerned. Once he had left the village there was no way back.

The other way of escape was known as manumission. This involved paying the lord for one's freedom, and a heavy fine was usually exacted in return for granting it. I have not found a single instance of either manumission or escape from any Gamlingay manor, but it must have happened. The lack of manorial documents from the Woodbury and Avenel manors (the ones with the unfree tenants) is the cause of the silence.

What the villein received in return for his hefty services and obligations seems almost ludicrous in comparison: a hovel, a few miserable acres of land and the dubious benefit of his lord's protection. This was the essence of the feudal system: land in return for service. It permeated downwards from the king, at the apex of the feudal pyramid, to the broad mass of toiling peasantry at the base. It applied to the Sir John Avenels of the medieval world as much as to their villeins, although the Avenels' obligations consisted of providing fighting men for the king's armies rather than getting their hands dirty by labouring.

Compensations existed for the villein, of course. There is something appealing to modern minds in the idea of an outdoor life, however hard it may have been in reality, and I have no doubt that the villein had an infinitely better understanding and enjoyment of natural things

– animals, birds, landscape, the slow turning of the seasons – than we are ever likely to have. To many people, the thought of living in a society in which one knew one's obligations and had few responsibilities beyond living from day to day is an attractive one, no matter how unpalatable it actually was to many villeins at the time. And more concrete compensations arose which made the villein's lot a little less unhappy. Gradually the taxes and exactions came to be fixed by 'the custom of the manor', and in general the lords found it in their interests to keep to it. Disputes were settled in the manor court by reference to custom. Fines for entering a holding were fixed by custom. Even the way the parish land was used was fixed by custom.

In the long run, establishing the custom of the manor came to benefit the villagers more than it did the lords. For instance, once a rent was fixed it tended to stay fixed, sometimes for hundreds of years. Trusting to custom gave the villagers a solid, ultra-conservative framework in which to live. They knew what was expected of them and the lord knew what he was due. The village became set in its ways, even rather comfortable, containing the many opposing points of view as an old armchair comes in time to fit the shape of the person who usually sits in it. This led in turn to a distrust of change, especially in working practices, even when it was patently obvious that everyone would benefit. I once heard a foreigner remark 'do something the same way twice in England and they call it a tradition'. The origin of this truism lies buried deep in the heart of the medieval countryside, in the idea of 'the custom of the manor'.

Avenel, Sir Hugh de Babington and Merton College all claimed 'view of frankpledge', which simply means that for most of their tenants they dispensed the law in all but major cases of crime. They also claimed 'assize of bread and ale', meaning that they controlled the weight and quality of those two staples of medieval diet, although 'nobody knows by what right they claim' as the Rolls put it. That legal nicety did not deter them because they went on dispensing their 'justice' for hundreds of years. The reason behind their apparently disinterested involvement with the law was money. In fining wrong-doers or in coming down hard on brewers of bad ale and sellers of underweight bread they were putting a little more cash in their manorial coffers.

Sir John Avenel also claimed the right to hold a market in the village every Tuesday. In the thirteenth century many villages – or more accurately, their lords – gained the right to hold markets. Most were small affairs, like Sir John's, and never amounted to very much: a few itinerant traders and a villager or two with some surplus produce to sell. It brought a few more pennies to Sir John by way of tolls, and doubtless the villagers enjoyed the chance to gossip with their neighbours and friends, but to be a real success a market needed a strong and energetic lord behind it, which Sir John Avenel and his descendants never were. His Tuesday market, like others, struggled on until the economic upheavals of the sixteenth century killed it off. His market-place remains to this day, now the small car park of the Hardwicke Arms public house.

The village also boasted two windmills (then a recent invention) which stood on high ground to the south of the village, soon named 'Mill Hill'. One was owned by Merton College, the other by the Abbot of Sawtry. The windmills made redundant the watermill which was part of Sir John Avenel's manorial complex, a fact that probably accounts for its non-appearance in the Hundred Rolls. Villeins were expected to grind their corn at their lord's mill, despite the fact they could do it more cheaply by using small hand-querns at home. The lord took his share of the flour of course. Even so, for free tenants with more corn to grind than the villeins, convenience might dictate that they used the windmill too.

The Hundred Rolls reveal that rents were often paid in kind as well as cash: William de Welles paid 3s. 7d. yearly for his house, a ten-acre close, twenty-four acres of arable land and an acre of meadow. In addition he had to find 'one pound of cumin and half a pound of pepper'. Adam son of Simon paid cash and one capon for his land and house, while Nigel de Mimmes paid for his two-acre croft by maintaining 'one candle before the altar of the Blessed Mary in Gamelinge, price 25d.'. And the following goes some way towards restoring one's faith in humanity:

Alice de Scalar holds six acres of land from Merton and renders for it each year *one flowering rose*.

By 1279 even the humblest villein had acquired a surname. Villeins had always had Christian names, of course, and probably surnames, although nobody had bothered to record them. The problems caused by half a dozen Johns or Simons in one village must soon have led to some form of distinguishing terminology, but possibly not to a system of inherited surnames. Even in 1279 surnames were, to a certain extent, still in a state of flux. Some are straightforward: Malin of the Church, William the Clerk, Gregory Est and Cecilia the daughter of the smith all present few problems. Some are based on occupations: Simon Baker, William Miller, John Tiler, Simon Carpenter and John Cook. Others must have developed from nicknames, like Agnes Red, Richard Prune, Philip Chikin and the unfortunate Custance Balde. I admit that 'John Human' does puzzle me somewhat (and Oda Flie more than somewhat). And where did 'Orabile de Hattele' get his name? Most Christian names among the men tend to be the everyday Williams, Johns, Simons and Thomases. The womenfolk were likewise limited to the commonplace Margarets, Matildas, Emmas and Sarahs.

2

The Manor

Of the three manors in the parish of Gamlingay, Merton is the only one for which any detailed documentation survives. Therefore most of what I shall have to say about the next 200 years will be based on Merton's records, mostly bailiffs' accounts and manor court rolls. Those of the court will concern us later, but the bailiffs' accounts, which run almost continuously from 1279 throughout the Middle Ages and on into the sixteenth century, give us an opportunity to examine the innermost workings of a manor in detail.

Apart from the land they rented out, lords usually retained a large acreage for their own use. This was called 'demesne land'. The College managed its manor and demesne through a bailiff, who had sole charge of day-to-day affairs but who was responsible to the steward, and, ultimately, to the warden of the College himself. The bailiff ran the estate with the aid of his servants and his labourers, and it was he who had to face the auditors when they arrived to check his accounts on their annual circuit of College property. If the bailiff had made a profit for his employers on the year's work he could face his inquisitors with a clear conscience, but if he had made a loss he probably awaited them with some trepidation — after all, he could be forced to make good the difference out of his own pocket.

The bailiff wrote the accounts himself if he could; if he could not, then a hired clerk did it for him. They were written on narrow strips of parchment sewn together to form one long roll, usually wound around a piece of wood for easy handling. Normally the accounts contain an entry recording the cost of this parchment, some of which was used by the manor court as well. At the top of the roll the clerk entered the name of the bailiff and the year covered by the accounts, which usually ran from the July of one year to the July of the next. Then, after listing various arrears due from the previous year, the sources of revenue were noted – rents, profits from the manor court, money raised from the sale of stock, cereals, meadows and so on – along with sundry items of other income. The revenue was added up, totalled, and then the expenses were listed: upkeep of the ploughs and carts, the mill, the manorial buildings, the cost of harvesting, wages and so forth, until they too were totalled up, a balance drawn and the year's profit or loss declared. There is frequently an inventory tacked on to the end of the accounts listing the manorial stock, the corn remaining in the granary and the household goods and equipment.

Medieval records are very difficult to read at first, but with a little practice and a lot of patience one can soon learn to distinguish individual letters, then complete words. These documents are written in a highly abbreviated form of Latin, with scarcely two words in ten written out in full. Fortunately the clerks who compiled them were often as vague about the strict rules of Latin grammar as I am.

As for what the accounts have to tell us, it is as well to remember that a manor was a business, run like any other, to make a profit. Quite literally everything is recorded and accounted for, down to the last farthing. To print even one of these accounts in all its fantastic detail would tax the staying-power of anyone who is not a qualified accountant. From the point of view of this story many interesting details that are fascinating in themselves cannot be included here, being strictly the province of the economic historian. I can, however, quote some which shed light on everyday manorial life.

The cluster of manorial buildings stood in a close next to the brook, facing on to the Hatley Road. In the centre of the close stood one of the largest and best-appointed houses in the entire village: the manor house, home of the bailiff. It was surrounded by the sort of buildings familiar enough on farms until relatively recently – the tithe granary, the great granary, smaller barns, hen-houses, pigsties, cowsheds, cattle sheds, sheep-pens, dairy, dovehouse (keeping doves was another manorial right), butchery and, later on at any rate, a steeping-house and kiln, both for malt. There was also a house for the manorial workers, known as the 'famuli', needed to run such a large establishment: shepherd, cowherd, swineherd, gooseherd, carters, drovers, ploughmen, dairymaid, etc. Nearer to the bailiff's house stood the

Merton manor

kitchen, separated from it because of the risk of fire, and a kitchen garden full of herbs and vegetables. Furthest from the road stood the L-shaped fishpond, stocked with carp and other edible freshwater fish. It is still there, filled in and overgrown, one of the many enigmatic 'moats' marked on Ordnance Survey maps. The whole estate was surrounded by a clay wall covered with thatch.

The bailiff's house was a typical medieval open-hall house. That is, the main room – the hall – was open to the roof, but the two end sections were of two storeys and housed the 'services'. Most reference books that deal with open-hall houses comment on the hole in the roof above the hall through which the smoke from the central hearth

escaped. Such an arrangement was plainly not good enough for a
bailiff of refinement like Richard de Bredon, because in 1345/6 he had
three carpenters make a 'louvre on the camera'. 'Camera' in this sense
means chamber, or house. The louvre was probably no more than a
hole in the roof; the next entry clarifies what I mean by refinement:

One barrel bought for the louvre – 4d.

It is not immediately obvious, but if you knock out the ends of a barrel
you are left with something that resembles a chimney. Insert it in the
hole in the roof and you have a rather desirable convenience lacking
in most contemporary village houses.

There are dozens of entries concerning repairs done to the bailiff's
house, but three examples taken from the period 1280–1350 will
suffice here.

1281/2
Wages of one mending the roof of the house and roofing the gatehouse at
piecework – 11d.

1330/31
Wages of one carpenter making a new solar door and other necessary work
for two days – 5d.

1347/8
One carpenter hired for ten days making a vault in the solar, 'les steires', four
gates and other necessary work . . . 2s. 6d.

A solar was an upstairs room, hence the need for stairs. But what was
the bailiff's house like inside? We can get a good idea from a precious
inventory made in 1314 after the death of John de Senkeworth. He had
'farmed' (leased) the whole manor from Merton in 1302. When he
died twelve years later the College made the most detailed inventory
I have ever seen.

Let us take a stroll around the manorial complex in the company
of the scribe who wrote the inventory. He began, naturally enough,
with the house itself, and with the most important part of it, the hall.
In it he found a trestle table, a basin and ewer, a bench, a chair and
two stools. This rather spartan room was where the manor court was
held. No doubt the steward and his clerk spread their rolls of parchment on the trestle table while the rest of the court stood, sat on the

floor or fought for the few seats available. The pantry was also in the house, in the service area. It contained more or less what you would expect a medieval pantry to contain. There were a couple of cloths, a bread-basket and a lamp; a few casks, some for wine and some for salt; a flour-basket, and a chest made of fir and 'bound with iron'. There were also fourteen wooden cups for the manorial workers, and a flour-sieve.

In John de Senkeworth's private room – or rooms, since the following items were probably divided between his parlour (downstairs) and his solar (upstairs) – were his personal effects. The rooms were hung with tapestries, and here he kept his most valued possessions, with a strong lock or two on the doors and chests to keep them safe. They contained, among other things:

One red cloak worth 2s.
One silk shirt – 18d.
One calico robe – 2s. 6d.
One white corset – 18d.
One russet tunic – 18d.
Three gold rings worth 18d.
Shears worth 2d.
One knife – 3d.
One strongbox – 3s.
Two mazers, one of which has a silver stand – 7s.
Four silver spoons – 3s. 2d.
One sword – 8d.
White leather and one purse – 3d.
Two books of romance worth 3d.
Pepper worth 3d.
Oil worth 6d.
Two embroidered linen cloths – 12d.
One gold clasp ornamented with silver pennies and one small clasp – 20d.

Those books intrigue me: what were they? Not romance in the modern sense, but stories of knights and chivalry. Apart from the church, John de Senkeworth's house was the only one to contain a book. And what would those handwritten books be worth today? More than 3d, certainly.

So much for the house. Outside it stood the lesser buildings. The dairy had its cheese-moulds and cloths, and three 14-foot-long shelves laden with ripening cheeses. The kitchen had its oven, a great brass cauldron, jar, pitcher, measures, brass bowls, knife, chopping board, 'boket', twenty-six plates, sixty dishes, twelve saucers and other paraphernalia. Littered around the various granaries, barns, stables and suchlike were all the implements needed to run a farm. There were forks and spades, mattocks, pecks and scythes; there were ladders lying around for the unwary to trip over, there were ploughs to bump into, horse harnesses and ox harnesses to fall over, carts, horseshoes, nails, pans, cloths, axes, ropes – the detail is simply amazing. The scribe also noted the amount of grain left in the barns, which was not very much, since the inventory was compiled in June, just before the harvest got well under way.

The manorial livestock is not forgotten either. Eleven cows are listed, a careful distinction being made between those worth 7s. each and those only worth 5s., along with two bulls, one young bull, three heifers and three calves. Eighty sheep are noted at 16d. each; they were folded on the fields so their dung would fertilise the soil. There were also six hoggets, twenty-nine wethers and twenty-seven lambs. Three horses are valued at 50s. each, and nine oxen at 14s. each. Horses were more valuable than the workaday oxen, and were used mainly for transport, while oxen were left to pull the great ploughs and the heavy carts. Three steers, forty pigs, two sows and fifteen piglets complete the list.

This picture of a medieval farm would not be complete without some poultry clucking and flapping their way around the yard and, sure enough, they were listed too:

Three unmated geese.
Thirteen goslings.
One cock.
Twelve chickens.

In a later section of the inventory nine goslings make an appearance, but then counting poultry always was a notoriously difficult business.

The accounts proper can often give one a better idea of the farm buildings. When in 1358/9 Merton decided to build a new barn a master carpenter called Geoffrey Silvestre was employed to do the work. Here are a few extracts from the account:

Paid to Geoffrey Silvestre, carpenter, by agreement, for all carpentry work about one new barn in length 160 feet, and for making three doors for the said barn − £6 13s. 4d. and one quarter of wheat and one quarter of malt.

Carriage of wood from another barn bought by the Warden − 3s.

Same carpenter for making five ladders for the said barn − 3s.

Two men for twenty days working for hire to level the ground for the new barn and the stables, 3d. per day − 10s.

8000 'latchnayls' bought − 13s. 4d.

900 'spikyngnayl' bought − 3s. 9d.

Paid Simon Selkman for 36,000 tiles; in part payment for 12,000 he had thirty cartloads of firewood, and for the rest the price per thousand was 6s.

Building a barn some 53 yards long was quite an undertaking. It sounds as if an old barn was bought and the wood cannibalised to make a new one, but normally most of the timber used about the manor came from Merton Wood. Dr Rackham in his book *Trees and Woodland in the British Landscape* (Dent, London, 1976) estimated that at least 561 trees of various sizes were taken from Merton Wood between 1333 and 1337 − a prodigious amount.

When the brand-new barn stood with its doors wide open ready to welcome the first sheaves of corn, there was always plenty more work for the carpenters, thatchers, tilers, plasterers and labourers to do. Running a manor farm involved endless repair and building. There were walls to erect, ditches to dig, ploughs to mend, carts to fix. The following are a few extracts from the regular expenses, taken at random. There are thousands of others.

1281/2
Upkeep of ploughs:
Six pieces of iron bought − 18d.
Two-and-a-half sheaves of steel − 2s.
Four halters − 1d.
Carpenter repairing wood about the ploughs − 13$\frac{1}{2}$d.
The smith's wages − Michaelmas to Easter − 2s. 2d.
Repairing one ploughshare − 1d.
Upkeep of carts:
One pair of wheels with an axle − 2s. 2d.

Canvas bought to mend the cart collars – 2½d.
Repairing three new collars and mending two old ones – 5½d.
Fourscore and ten great nails – 10½d.
Four bands to go around the wheel-hubs – 1½d.
Oil and grease – 1d.
Repairs to three carts – 2d.

1326/7
Wages of one carpenter for *removing one house from the vill to the manor*, and there rebuilding it – 10s. 6d. by agreement.
For one to plaster and wattle and daub same house, and for roofing it – 6s. 4d. by agreement.
Wattling and roofing the steeping-house – 4s.
Thatching the tithe-barn – 18d.

1345/6
Two carpenters hired for eleven days to make a new beam for the kiln, a door and a stall for the stable, and making a stall and mending a stall and other work in the ox-house and barns – 4s. 7d.

1358/9
Building a new kitchen: all carpentry work including studding and plastering the walls, and one man hired to tile the said kitchen . . . 36s.

And then there was always the mill. This was (or these were – there were lots of them) a post mill, a wooden structure balanced on a central post so it could be turned to face the wind. It was a constant source of expense. It stood on its mill-mound at the southern end of the village, and when it was working it must have been a splendid sight with its canvas-covered sails revolving in the breeze. When it was not working – which was quite often, in fact – the College must have cursed the new-fangled contraption. Medieval mills were very unreliable; Merton had to replace theirs every fifteen or twenty years. Building a new one was a large operation which involved almost every able-bodied man the manor could muster.

1279
For scouring the ditch and raising the mill-mound – 12d.
For ditches at 'Stocking' [a field name] from where earth was carted to make the mill-mound – 2s. 8d.

Making a mill-mound was a tremendous task. In 1341/2 Merton paid
1½d. each to *251* men working to repair the mill-mound. What an
effort! This was probably considered to be part of the villeins' customary service; if not, I imagine they were 'expected' to lend a hand.

When a new mill was built the old one had to be demolished and
a new central post put in. This was a massive piece of oak some 2 feet
square and 20 feet long, weighing about 2 tons, which had to be
securely fixed in order to take the weight of the mill structure. This
example is from 1295/6:

Carpenter to make the new mill – 40s. and a quarter of wheat.
He and another carpenter for two days lifting the mill – 16d.
Ten men to remove the old post from the ground – 20d.
Fourteen men to ram in the new post and for other work about the mill –
2s. 4d.

Between times the mill required constant attention in the battle against the elements. This is a selection from hundreds of similar items:

1287/8
22 small pieces of iron for the axle and wheel – 13¼d.
Wood for the axle and wheel – 7d.

1288/9
30 ells of canvas for the sails – 6s. 0¼d.
One basket – 2¼d.

1289/90
Wooden mill-measure – 21d.
Mill-post – 18s.
Carpentry work about the post, and placing it in position – 8s.
One axle – 1s. 0¼d.
Bills made and repaired – 10d.
Oil bought – 4d.

1333/4
4 men working during harvest cutting and removing the foundations of the post so the Warden could see the damage – 3s.
400 'spykyngs' – 12d.
Wages of the smith making two plates to go around the axle and one circular bridge on the head of the post, along with the iron purchased – 15d.
2 men carrying water for the clay used to ram in the post – 12d.
Expenses of the carpenter and three of his servants: in bread 1½d., ale 2½d., meat 3¼d., and a goose from stock.
Mending a cable broken when bringing in the post – 3d.
Iron rings on the mill sails – 8d.

So it went on, year in, year out. Millstones wore out, joints gave way, sails ripped and axles broke, all of which were things the bailiff could reasonably put down to normal wear and tear. In 1303/4, however, neither wear and tear nor bad workmanship could be blamed:

Making one new axle and placing it in Gamelyngey mill – 2s.
Afterwards a great wind blew at night and broke and threw down two sailyards and the said new axle; therefore, for new sailyards and a new axle – 4s.

Sometimes, as in 1340/41, the destruction was deliberate:

Sending a servant to Oxford in order to know what to do with the miller for burning the mill – 6d.

What the warden said about his pyromaniac miller is not recorded. Perhaps it is just as well.

Other expenses around the manor occurred more normally. Merton College were rectors of the church, and claimed the 'great tithes' of the parish. The lesser tithes were claimed by the vicar. Great tithes included those of hay, corn and wood – hence the tithe barn in which they were kept appears often in the accounts. In return the College was responsible for the upkeep of the chancel, while the rest of the building was repaired and renewed by the parishioners. Here are some examples of the expenses this involved.

1303/4
Roofing the chancel – 2s. $2\frac{1}{2}$d.
One white linen cloth – 2s. $10\frac{1}{2}$d.
For a lamp to burn incense in, and for repairing vestments – $7\frac{1}{4}$d.
Lime bought, sand dug, and wages of workmen mending the chancel windows – $4\frac{1}{2}$d.

1306/7
Glass for the chancel windows and glazier's wages – 15d.
Book-binding – 4d.

1324
5 pieces of iron for the church windows – 20d.
For bell-clappers and their carriage – 13d.
Carpenter making the 'celyng' in the chancel, in part payment – 4s.
Repairing lead – 4d.

1334
Making a lock for the chancel door – 2d.

The church was one of the few buildings in the village – perhaps the only one – to have glazed windows. They must have been a tempting target for small boys, judging by the number of times they were mended.

The aspects of medieval life known to almost everyone are the traditional punishments for minor offences: the ducking-stool (properly 'cucking-stool') for garrulous women, the pillory and the tumbril. These are the only references to them I have found:

1298/9
Two carpenters making a byre, a pillory and a ducking-stool . . . 8s.

1334
For the man who made 'le Thew' and 'le Tumberell', 14d. by agreement.

'Thew' seems to be another word for a ducking-stool. There was a darker side to the use of the ducking-stool: it was a remnant of the earlier practice of trial by water. A tumbril was a muck cart with a backboard that could be let down to tip the contents out. Carting a miscreant around in a tumbril was meant to imply that he or she was no better than the usual contents.

The accounts teem with so many unclassifiable items of manorial expenditure that the clerks often jumbled them all together under the heading of 'sundries'. Here are a few of them, quoted to illustrate the way even the smallest costs were noted down and accounted for:

1280
Tallow for the year, 15lb for $18\frac{1}{2}$d.

1281/2
Grease and verdigris for the sheep-scab − 5d.
Leeks bought to plant in the yard − 6d.

1288/9
Cleaning a ditch behind the garden, which was previously stopped up to the nuisance of the whole vill − 26d.

1298/9
Two servants hired to remove the timber from one old house *blown down* – 3d.
Making 36 hurdles for the fold – 7d.
Two pans of pike purchased – 1½d.

1329/30
Castrating eight young pigs – 3d.
Digging a ditch at the head of 'le fyschpond' – 3s. 4d.

1333/4
Two pounds of candles bought for visiting the animals at night . . . 4d.

And so on. Finally, there is one further area of life in the Middle Ages that is illuminated by these accounts: bribery. This did more than just oil the wheels; for underpaid and overworked officials of the lower ranks bribes constituted a large part of their income, while higher officials could easily make a fortune. We find an example of 'oiling the wheels' when in 1312/3 our friend John de Senkeworth gave half a quarter of oats worth 1s. 3d. to the mayor of Cambridge 'in order that he be favourable in taxing household goods'. Sometimes the bailiff was uncertain whether a bribe was required or not. This is William Cokinho in 1332/3:

Servant carrying a letter to Oxford to ask Warden's advice about taking corn for the king's use . . . 6d.

This refers to the system of purveyance, whereby the king's representatives were empowered to demand cheap food and goods for the royal household, a system that inevitably led to many disputes. In this instance the necessary advice was evidently sent because the next time the royal purveyors called at the manor there was no hesitation:

1334/5
To the king's bailiff, 3s. 4d. for not taking corn for the king.

And 3s. 4d. seems to have become the standard bribe the purveyors could expect every time they knocked at the manorial gates.

I wish it were possible to know *how* these accounts, in all their incredible detail, were actually compiled. Did the bailiff keep notes on scraps of parchment and write them up at the year's end? Or did he and the reeve (his foreman) bring out their tally sticks, check the notches cut in convenient beams in the granaries and barns, and strain their memories to recall the income and expenditure for the year? It beats me. But I can tell you how much the clerks who usually wrote the accounts up on behalf of the bailiff received for their trouble, because the amount is diligently recorded every year: anything from 2 to 8s. per account.

Apart from one or two short periods when it was leased, Merton manor was run by a bailiff until the early 1360s. From then on, the estate was permanently leased to a farmer. The accounts proper dry up, to become a short recital of virtually fixed annual expenses on the estate. The College, naturally enough, did not need to know all the details of the farmer's business, and as time goes on the interest of the accounts fades.

3

The Manor Court

Each year the bailiff's accounts contain a record of the profits of the manor courts, usually amounting to a few shillings from each sitting. The court was held by the steward of Merton, who rode out from Oxford on his circuit of College manors. He carried with him the court rolls on which the proceedings of past courts were written, which was useful when it came to establishing the 'custom of the manor'. When this important personage arrived to lodge at the bailiff's house he expected to be entertained in a suitably lavish style – no pottage or black rye-bread for him. The cost of the visit was, as you will expect by now, duly entered in the accounts. During one visit in 1333/4 the steward consumed bread, ale, beef, mutton, mustard, candles, six capons and a piglet, as well as a bushel of oats for his horse.

Courts were held regularly from at least 1279; court rolls survive from 1340. They do not run continuously, however. The first batch to survive span the years 1340 to 1355 (significant years, as we shall see), and they will be the ones to concern us here. Like the bailiff's accounts, court rolls were written in heavily abbreviated dog-Latin.

The room in which the court sat (the bailiff's hall) was packed with tenants anxious to see the day's business concluded. While the jury was being sworn in the clerk was busy noting down the details of date and place of the court, sometimes finding time to embellish the capital letters. Then he entered the names of the jury, those who sent their excuses for non-attendance (the 'essoins'), and those who did not, who were fined 2 or 3d. for their dilatoriness. After these formalities, the court settled down to business. In fact, there should have been two courts, a court leet and a court baron, but things had become rather relaxed and the courts combined.

Reading a series of court rolls covering a long period of time soon reveals that certain cases crop up with monotonous regularity. The records of well over a hundred courts survive between 1340 and the early sixteenth century, and at each court entries like the following ones appear:

1346
The jury present that William Warde, fined 8d., John Reve, 2d., Alan Basse, 8d., John Basse, 8d., Walter the clerk, 4d., Robert Yarker, 3d., Henry Wolf, 8d., William Sped, 1d., John Warde, 6d., William Cord, 3d., Emma Sped, 8d., and John le Rede, 4d., are brewers who sold ale contrary to the assize. And that Rose Speed, fined 1d., did likewise.

The jury present that John Basse, fined 4d., and Alice Sentere, fined 2d., are bakers who sold contrary to the assize.

The assize of bread and ale – the statutory regulations concerning price and quality – created the need for special manorial officers called aletasters. Working in pairs, they had the task of sampling the new brew of each alehouse. The brewer fixed the traditional ale-stake at the front of his dwelling when he (or she – many were women) wished the aletasters to call. It will come as no surprise to learn that the post of aletaster was a very popular one indeed. Once secured, the job was often clung to with a tenacity that death alone could break; despite this, almost as frequent an entry as the offenders against the assize:

1346
John le Rede, fined 4d., and John Stalonn, fined 2d., are aletasters and did not do their duty.

Continual presentation for 'not doing their duty' does not seem to have deterred these public-spirited men. After all, a few pennies in fines was a small price to pay for the free ale they consumed at each brew. Neither do the fines the brewers paid seem to have made much difference to the quality of the drink they produced (the same can be said of the bakers and their bread), for the same people appear again and again before the court, continually being fined and continually transgressing. In reality, the fines had long since become a sort of licence-fee, and nobody pretended they were anything else. So long as they paid up, the village bakers and brewers could continue to trade; withdrawal of custom would deal with those who sold undrinkable ale or inedible bread. Just occasionally one finds a glimpse of humanity from the steward among the repetitive list of fines, as in these entries from 1340:

Presented that Godwyne (*pardoned because he is a pauper*) and Christian Malyn (fined 2d.) are regrators of ale who sold contrary to the assize.

Likewise Alan Basse baked bread and sold it contrary to the assize. *Pardoned because he is old.*

Another regular feature of court business was the transfer and inheritance of land and houses, and nearly all the rolls contain items like this:

1346
John Rykyld . . . came and showed that he holds of the lord one house with a croft adjacent and one-and-a-half acres of land by right of his wife, for services of 15d. per year, homage, fealty and suit of court.

Attendance at court ('suit of court') could count as one of a villein's day-works. Sometimes a dispute arose from these land and house transfers, and the jury was asked to settle the matter according to the time-honoured 'custom of the manor'. In 1344 the jury were told that Alan atte Hoo, who held a house and ten acres of land in bondage tenure, had died;

and the whole homage swear that by the custom of the manor his wife should hold the property for the term of her life *without paying the entry fine*. And she gives in heriot one heifer worth 3s.

Money, of course, was the reason why lords held courts. There was a profit to be made from justice, as little Alice Basse discovered in 1340:

It was ordered at the previous court to seize into the lord's hands Alice the daughter of William Basse, along with a house and croft, because she is under age. And now comes John the son of Walter who gives the lord 13s. 4d. as a dowry. Pledge the bailiff.

The previous court had been told Alice was to be 'seized' because her father was dead and she was under age, 'namely, under eleven years'. Since she was under age Merton were entitled to play the part of surrogate father and pocket the dowry. Her husband-to-be, of course, simply wanted her property. Before any reader chokes with indignation I had better point out that child marriages were relatively rare but not unknown in medieval England.

In a similar vein, lords of the manor could fine their female tenants for what seems at first sight a rather odd offence.

1346
Alice, late the wife of Alan atte Hoo, committed Letherwyt with William Norys junior. Therefore it is ordered to seize the whole tenement which Alice holds from the lord in bondage.

Letherwyt (or lairwite) was incontinence, or in plain English, illicit sexual intercourse. It seems strange that Merton College, as an absentee landlord, should concern itself with the moral behaviour of its tenants. Indeed, the particularly harsh punishment would seem to indicate strong disapproval of Alice atte Hoo and her lover. But, as usual in manorial affairs, practical economics was at the root of the matter. The clue lies in the fact that Alice held her late husband's property in bondage tenure, which meant that legally she herself was a chattel of the College. Therefore, in running the risk of pregnancy and her consequential inability to perform her manorial services she was held to be damaging the lord's property. The first time she had been found guilty of letherwyt (in 1345) she got away with a 2s. fine. This time she lost her land and house. They were taken because it was a condition of her right to hold them that she remained unmarried and chaste. The only defence I can offer on behalf of the College is that Alice atte Hoo's case is the only one recorded in the entire manor court-rolls. But before one gives too much credit to Merton for not pursuing other erring women it is as well to bear in mind that the 'crime' of letherwyt only applied to bond women, and the majority of the College tenantry was free.

Much more common are entries like these:

1347
Andrew Russell is placed in the tithing of Alan Melleward and sworn.

Robert the son of William Norys is placed in the tithing of William Chyken and sworn.

John Cokerel has remained in the lord's fee for a year and more and is not in a tithing. Fined 1d.

These regular entries record an ancient method of keeping the peace. When a boy reached the age of twelve he was enrolled in a tithing, a group of households (nominally ten) under the watchful eye of a chief tithingman. Similarly, any newcomer to the village was expected to join his local tithing. The chief tithingmen usually formed the jury of the court, and were held responsible for the good behaviour of their tithing. Failing to enrol in a tithing produced a few more pennies towards the profits of the court.

Considering that the manor court dealt with many petty transgressions it is surprising to find that theft does not seem to have been a very common occurrence. Cases like this are few and far between:

1346
John Latewys stole corn at night. Fined 10d.

This may be due to the fact that in a close-knit community the chances of getting away with a crime were small; or it may be that the victim and his friends exacted their own form of punishment without recourse to the manor court. The victim in most of the cases recorded seems to have been the College itself.

1346
John le Rede took a cart to fetch his grain in on six occasions without licence from the bailiff. Fined 12d.

And he took the lord's plough without licence to plough his land. Fined 12d.

And he depastured the lord's pasture with his beasts. Fined 12d.

Some entries are more cryptic. In 1347 Alice Draper was fined 3d. for 'damaging the lord's estate'. How did she damage the lord's estate? We are not told, but presumably it was by letting her cattle roam unchecked.

Wandering animals were a problem. Any that were found at large within the manor boundaries were claimed by the lord as 'waifs and strays', and so one finds occasionally, as in 1353, the jury saying that 'one horse weyf came into the lord's demesne and is valued at 12d.'. Another little mystery exists there: why was the horse only worth 1s.? It should have been valued at fifteen or twenty times as much. Perhaps 1s. was the fine the owner had to pay to get his horse back, because, of course, pay a fine he must. If nobody claimed the animal it became College property.

Before we leave the court rolls for a while, here are a few of the cases which took up the valuable time of the steward and the jury. They are offered without comment.

1347
Henry the son of William Dorlyng took and carried off the lord's corn contrary to his wish. Fined 2d.

John le Taillour of Lolworth has bought a house from Thomas Croke. Ordered to distrain him to show by what right he holds.

1348
Richard Pope's daughter and Isabella Ingyl badly gleaned the corn in harvest. Fined 3d. each.

1352

Deonis Basse (2d.) John Dyxwelle (1d.) and Margaret Spede (2d.) for not bringing their measures to court.

John Wattesone damaged the lord's corn with two horses. Damage estimated at half a bushel of barley. Fined 2d.

John the son of William Stywe damaged the lord's corn with twenty sheep. Fined 2d.

1352

Ordered to distrain Simon Tullok before the next court to answer John le Smyth in plea of debt.

With the advantage of hindsight it is possible to see the thirteenth and fourteenth centuries as a watershed in both manorial and medieval prosperity. An increasing population during the thirteenth century led to a corresponding increase in the amount of land under cultivation. Larger markets and a servile workforce meant increased wealth for the owners of land. But the decline from this peak of prosperity was already under way during the first half of the fourteenth century. Stagnation had set in, and a shuddering blow was about to fall on an unwary people. It is an event that deserves a chapter to itself.

4

Death is Like a Shadow

Scratched on a pier in Gamlingay church in a large, unmistakably medieval hand are the words '*mors comparat umbre, que semper sequitur corpus*'. Translated they mean 'death is like a shadow, which always follows a body'. The anonymous writer of this sad little truism, almost certainly a priest, was, I believe, prompted to record his feelings because he had just witnessed the awesome calamity of 1349, known to posterity as the Black Death. It is the only monument to the scores of villagers who perished in its wake.

The first and most devastating of the many plagues to infect England arrived from the continent via the south coast ports late in 1348 and spread rapidly across the country during the mild winter that followed. The very mildness of the weather aided its progress, for the rat-fleas which carried the disease were normally dormant during the winter months. Rats, common everywhere in both town and country, infested the filthy hovels of the village and the congested streets of the town, so that, once started, the disease travelled quickly from place to place. It was no contest, this battle between a panic-stricken populace and the bacterium *Pasturella pestis*. The consequence to the infected was a swift but very painful death. In its more usual form the disease caused swelling and haemorrhaging around the lymph glands, and a 70 per cent death rate was normal among those who contracted it. Another, more virulent form, was passed directly from person to person in the air. Death in this case was an absolute certainty within four days. Neither the English people nor anyone else was equipped – medically or psychologically – to deal with it. They were helpless, and they knew it.

The tide of death reached Cambridgeshire around April of 1349, and one can only speculate on the effect that the news of the approaching menace had on the villages in its path. Some parishes, like Elsworth and Great Shelford, seem to have escaped the disaster completely. Others, like Gamlingay, were not so lucky.

Most of the evidence I have to offer about the effect of the Black Death on the village comes from the court rolls we are already familiar with. The following is a brief summary of that evidence.

a) I have said that aletasters held on to their jobs year after year. During 1349 and 1350 three new ones were elected, and at two courts only one aletaster served instead of the normal two.

b) Robert Godewyn, vicar for ten years, was replaced in April 1349 by Thomas Amys. In December 1349 Amys was replaced by John Chiken.

c) Between 1344 and 1348 seventy-six different surnames were mentioned in the court rolls. Of this number only thirty-two occur again in the rolls from 1349 to 1355, implying that 58 per cent of village families disappeared from the record.

d) Between 1344 and 1348, 112 individuals are named in the court rolls (after deleting those stated to have died). Only thirty of them are mentioned between 1349 and 1355. Some 73 per cent are never heard of again.

e) Using the lists of people fined for breaking the assize of bread and ale (because the same people appear again and again) I have calculated that between 1344 and 1348 twenty-six bakers and brewers make an appearance in the court rolls, after due allowance for those said to have died. Only seven appear again between 1349 and 1355. Once more, 73 per cent are never mentioned again.

f) The bailiff accounts for the years immediately following the Black Death are in a poor state of preservation, but it is possible to discern some entries relating to 'decayed rent' and to tenements 'lying vacant'.

g) Court-rolls survive only until 1355, when there is a temporary halt in the series. The record of the court held on 9 July 1349 (the first since the arrival of the plague) is filled with entries about property transfers, purchases of land and orders to distrain new landholders. The court held on 6 November 1349 is even more emphatic: twenty-three separate entries dealing with property and land transfers as opposed to the two or three in a normal court. Those entries tell the same sorry tale. Here is a typical one, from the July court.

Agnes Pope came and did fealty, and acknowledged that she holds from the lord half an acre in 'le forthend' following the death of her husband Richard Pope . . . for services of $1\frac{1}{2}$d. per annum. And she holds half an acre in the same place following the death of her sister Alice for services of 1d. per annum and two appearances at court. Therefore it is ordered to distrain Agnes to pay the entry-fine on the said half-acre she holds following the death of her sister Alice.

There are many other entries. Margaret the wife of Henry Rykyld comes to claim Henry's house and land because he is dead; so is William Henry; Margaret King, widow, claims a croft and two acres on behalf of her fatherless child; Thomas Basse, who held a house and nine acres of land, is dead — and so on. In 1352, three years after the event, one can still find entries like 'ordered to seize the late James Douglas's cottage for lack of a tenant'.

I think that this is convincing evidence of the arrival and the effects of the Black Death on the tenants of Merton manor. From its arrival in April 1349 until the cold weather set in during December the disease ravaged the parish, killing large numbers of men, women and children in a particularly nasty and painful way. How many perished it is impossible to say. Disappearing from the records is no proof of death, and taken in the context of what happened to the rest of England my percentages seem too high. Possibly many people took the opportunity to leave the village and start a new life somewhere else in the confusion that followed the arrival of the Black Death. But although my calculations refer only to Merton manor, a large proportion of villagers probably made an appearance sooner or later in the College records. Besides, it is inconceivable that the tenants of Merton suffered in isolation. If pressed, I would estimate that about half of the entire population of Gamlingay was killed by the plague during the terrible year of 1349. Set out in cold type like that it is easy to overlook what it must have meant to have half the village wiped out in a matter of months. Over England as a whole it is thought that about a third of the population died.

The after-effects of this catastrophe are still argued over by historians, but the indisputable facts are that the survivors demanded – and got – a higher wage for their labour, prices of agricultural produce fell and there was a general movement to accelerate the process of exchanging manorial services for rents and wages, which eventually led to the end of the manorial system in its purest form. On Merton manor the Black Death ensured that in the long run the manor was not profitable as a bailiff-run farm. After the next outbreak of plague in 1361 (about which, conversely, there is not one scrap of evidence in the Gamlingay records) the College leased it permanently to farmers. Commutation of services for rents and wages would not have affected Merton unduly with its free tenantry, but must have concerned the Woodbury and Avenel manors, both of which relied heavily on villein labour.

Given that the plague was a great disaster for the village, it is astonishing how quickly it recovered. Few tenements remained empty for long. The court rolls and bailiff's accounts for the following years show the speed with which things returned to something approaching normality. England just before the Black Death was a vastly over-populated country and could stand a large decrease in numbers (from an economic if not a humanitarian point of view), without too much land going out of cultivation. The survivors simply took on more land where they could. Other holdings had probably had too many people working them anyway.

The most violent shock, however, was undoubtedly psychological. Faith in the ultimate goodness of God was badly shaken. How, it was asked, could He allow this apparently indiscriminate slaughter of lord and villein, prince and pauper, priest and bishop? The behaviour of some parish priests seemed – to those who wished to find it – evidence of something very wrong with the Church. To put it bluntly, many priests ran away, leaving their parishioners without the support of the Church.

Strangely enough, the Church quickly recovered its lost prestige. Indeed, it gained a new vitality which exploded into the religious fervour of the following century. Hundreds of parish churches were wholly rebuilt, thousands of chantries and parish guilds were established and there was an upsurge in the numbers of people going on pilgrimages.

Everyday life settled down once more, although some of the rules had changed for ever. And yet, reaching out to us across the centuries since the village choked with the smell of rotting corpses and echoed with the agonised cries of the dying, is that simple heartfelt message to posterity scratched into the fabric of the church itself: 'death is like a shadow, which always follows a body'. It is not, so far as I can discover, a direct quotation, but it is a fitting epitaph to Richard Pope, Henry Rykyld, Thomas Basse and the rest who perished.

5

Those Who Mattered

So far in this story we have not been concerned with the upper branches of the manorial tree, but here we will have to step back and trace the history of the four main landholdings in the village because it is relevant to a proper understanding of the history of the village.

Merton manor remained, of course, Merton manor. Nor is there much to say about the Abbot of Sawtry's estate, known as 'Shackledon'. It was leased to various farmers until the dissolution of the monasteries. Avenel's, you may recall, was in the hands of John Avenel in 1279. From him it passed to his son William, who died in 1331, leaving the manor to his son John. This Sir John fought with Edward III in France during the Hundred Years' War, and died in Brittany in 1359, 'about the Gules of August', according to the inquisition post-mortem held after his death. This inquisition and the one held after his father had died in 1331 provide two rare glimpses of Avenel's manor.

As so often with rare or important documents, these two inquisitions are almost illegible, but they do yield a little information. In the first (1331) there is a hint that the Avenels were not the most enterprising family. It mentions the market, which, as I have said, ultimately failed because the Avenels did not push it hard enough, and that 'he [William Avenel] has pleas and profits of court there worth 2s.'. Compared to the roughly equivalent Merton manor, which in 1333 received 14s. 3d. from two courts, this sum of 2s. is a beggarly

35

Avenel's manor

amount. We are also told that the manor now possessed its own windmill. Sawtry and Merton had each had one as long ago as 1279.

The second inquisition post-mortem (1359) is equally frustrating; it looks as if a bottle of ink has been spilt on it, but at least we do learn that the windmill was worth 10s. a year (Merton leased theirs for twice that amount) and that the manor possessed two dovecotes worth 4s. 6d.

Those are virtually the only details of Avenel's manor I have found for the entire medieval period. The site still exists, a ploughed field now, with the moat in which water was stored to drive the watermill only recently filled in. The only remains of the manorial buildings are large areas of shattered peg-tiles, a few animal bones, some sherds of pottery and dozens of oyster-shells.

Meanwhile, the estate passed to yet another John. From him, in 1383, it went to Robert Avenel, who was the last of the line as things turned out. He married Gillian, the daughter of Sir Robert Bealknap, and died without leaving an heir. Sundry claimants to the estate appeared, with the Courteney family eventually emerging as victors from the ensuing legal tussles. They promptly sold the manor – by 1400 at the latest – to the impressively-named Sir Baldwin St George, who owned, and lived in, neighbouring Hatley St George, which took its name from his family. In a way, he was the ideal landlord: absentee, but not far away if needed. His widow inherited Avenel's in 1425, and then it went through the hands of his son Sir John, his son Sir William, and then to Sir Richard St George, who died in 1485. There is significance in the date: I believe he died at the battle of Bosworth. Sir Richard's son and heir Thomas St George was a minor, so custody of the estate was granted to the Archbishop of York. When Thomas came of age in 1494 he duly inherited the property.

Woodbury manor was in the hands of Sir Hugh de Babington in 1279. It remained Babington property, descending via Richard, Hugh, John, William (Chief Justice of the Common Pleas between 1423 and 1426) and another William, until this last William's son emulated Robert Avenel and died childless in 1501. Audrey Delves, his sister, inherited the manor. As with Avenel's and Shackledon there are virtually no surviving documents from Woodbury to tell the more interesting human side of the story, not even an ink-stained inquisition post-mortem. One is forced to rely on the records of Merton manor and assume that the affairs of the others were much the same: trespass, damage to property, debts, breaking the assize of bread and ale and so forth must have occurred as often on the manors we do not know about as on the one we do.

6

The Manor Court Again

The manor court rolls, those faithful mirrors of villagers' failings, start again in 1386 after a break of thirty years. Five years earlier the Peasant's Revolt of 1381 had taken place. As far as Gamlingay is concerned there is not one scrap of evidence to suggest the village was involved in any way – not the slightest hint of riot or the faintest whiff of burning. The court rolls of the following decades give no clues about the Revolt. Life on the manor went on much as usual, and as usual the bakers and brewers, defaulters, aletasters and sundry breakers of manorial rules paid their fines without having their muttered complaints recorded for posterity by the clerk.

However, there is a change in the tone of the rolls from now on. Gone is the strict manorial attitude towards services, heriots, merchet and the like, and in its place is a preoccupation with enforcing agricultural discipline and the proper management of village affairs. This would not have been necessary in the days of the rigid yet more community-minded manors of a hundred, or even fifty, years before. A marked increase in the number of cases dealing with debt is apparent during the next forty years. This sort of entry is typical:

1386
Ordered to attach John Neweman, smith, to answer William Chelestre in a plea of debt.

It is a noticeable feature of these rolls throughout their long history that at different periods the courts had different priorities. Over a number of years one finds dozens of cases all of a similar kind; people will be constantly fined for not cleaning their ditches properly, for instance, or else an upsurge in the number of assaults will preoccupy the court. During the late fourteenth and early fifteenth centuries the steward and his clerks must have been bored to distraction by the endless pleas of debt they were forced to hear. I should imagine that the everyday scenes of farmyard life visible through the window took on a more interesting aspect at such moments.

Trespass was another item which appeared again and again. At least the clerk was kept amused by the effort of spelling the many field names involved in the presentments. Here are some typical entries:

1407
Alexander Draper trespassed with his geese in the corn. Fined 12d.

John Yorke trespassed in the grain with his cow. Fined 2d.

1408
John Holewyn for trespass in the corn and pasture at 'le milledam'. Fined 10d.

1409
Henry Basse trespassed in 'Myllecroft' with his sheep. Fined 4d.

William Warde and John Peverell for trespass in 'le lays in le cornefeld'. Fined 2d. each.

How anyone could be so careless with their animals is beyond me. One is tempted to ask how the villagers managed to grow anything at all with so many valuable crops and resources destroyed by rampaging animals. The rise in the number of trespass cases is due to the hayward, a manorial official appointed to supervise the fences and enclosures which were supposed to prevent cattle straying, to look after the common stock, and to impound stray cattle. Any animals found wandering were locked up in the village pound until their contrite owners had paid the appropriate fine. As always, certain people were less willing than others to pay up:

1408

John Smith broke the lord's fold and took away his beasts contrary to the lord's wish. Fined 6d.

1417

William Warde, servant of John Fisher, broke the lord's pound and removed a horse taken for trespass in the lord's corn. Fined 2s.

Without a shadow of doubt William Warde was acting under orders from his master. The Fishers were a troublesome family, constant thorns in the flesh of Merton College during the fifteenth century, who took perverse pleasure in thumbing their noses at manorial authority. They were fined and admonished for one misdemeanour after another, and just as often they ignored both. Their attitude slowly became more widespread and symptomatic of England as a whole during the troubled times of the Wars of the Roses. This is a selection of typical entries concerning the family over a period of seventeen years:

1408

Hugo Fyssher owes suit of court – defaulted – fined 2d. His servant Walter not in tithing. Hugo Fyssher fined 2d.

Reginald Fysshere – trespass – horses in lord's corn and pasture. Fined 3d. Also geese in lord's corn. Fined 2d.

Thomas Fyssher – trespass – horses in lord's corn. Fined 4d.

1409

Reginald Fyscher distrained – plea of debt.

Thomas Fyscher – trespass – lord's wood on four occasions. Fined 12d.

Reginald Fyscher – trespass – pigs and animals in lord's wood and meadow. Fined 6d.

1413

Thomas Fyscher – default – fined 2d.

John Fyscher not in tithing. Fined 3d. Also trespass – farmer's corn twice. Fined 4d.

John the servant of Thomas Fyscher, on the orders of Thomas, placed horses in the farmer's pasture, broke the pound, and trespassed in the farmer's corn. Thomas fined 12d.

1414

Thomas and John Fysshere fined 2d. each for default.

Thomas Fyssher trespassed seven times in the lord's wood with his animals. Fined 2s. 4d. Also trespassed in the lord's rye. Fined 2d. And in the lord's meadow. Fined 3d.

John Fisher not in tithing. Ordered to be placed in one.

1425

John Fisssher has newly built a road across the lord's meadow in 'le brokende' to his house across the brook. Must amend it before All Saint's day on pain of fine of 3s. 4d.

That is just a selection, remember. I have to admit to a grudging admiration for the way the Fishers flouted authority, and also to much sympathy with the poor officials who had to try and deal with them. The Fishers, and hundreds of other families like them, were asserting their independence and individuality, and in doing so were hastening the end of the Middle Ages. In a century or two they would be commemorated and sentimentalised as the 'yeoman of England', but I do not suppose that either they, or the people who got in their way, saw it quite like that at the time.

Another area of constant dispute was that of encroachment in one form or another. The open fields, with their easily portable boundary marks, must always have been a sore temptation to the unscrupulous. An extra foot or two of soil grabbed from your neighbours' plot might easily go unnoticed. A couple of examples will suffice to show what was going on:

1414

Thomas Scot encroached on William Chastelet's land in length 4 perches and in width 2 feet. Fined 2s., and ordered to amend it before the next court on pain of 10s.

1422

John Welised senior encroached on the lord's land with a hedge one furlong in length and 2 feet and more in width. Ordered to remove it before the next court on pain of 10s.

All this is rather petty and uninspiring in comparison to the novel way Henry Mason found to annoy his neighbour in 1413:

Henry Mason has erected a house to the damage of John Symond. Ordered to distrain him before the next court.

How did Mason's house damage Symond? Was it built on Symond's land? Or did it merely obstruct his view, or his right of way? No: Mason's 'house' was a privy!

Occasionally the court ordered a tenant to build a new house as a condition of tenure. When Nicholas Wryght took over a house, garden and five acres in 1417 he was told to build 'a house with two rooms near the said house at his own expense before Michaelmas on pain of 20s. And the lord gives him timber suitable for splints and wattles or corbels to build it with. And in payment the lord gives him 23s. 4d.' One can only assume that this was done for one of two possible reasons: either the dwelling Nicholas Wryght was about to take over was on the verge of collapse, or else he had some relatives or servants he could not house. Given the state of some of the buildings in the village at this period the house was probably in ruins. Orders like this were not infrequent:

1391
Geoffrey Skynner has not repaired his house called 'le bakhous'. Fined 2d. Ordered to repair it before the next court on pain of 15d.

1412
John Ives was ordered at the last court to repair his ruinous tenement under pain of forfeit of 6s 8d. He has not done so; therefore the bailiff is ordered to levy the penalty.

As time went on this sorry state of affairs regarding village housing got worse rather than better, as we shall see.

Meanwhile wood, both firewood and timber for building purposes, was another of those valuable and shrinking manorial resources under constant threat from the unscrupulous and the needy. It could be said that woods and hedgerows were a communal asset to be used freely by all and sundry, but the deep ditch and earth wood bank which surrounded the wood (and still does today) argued differently. The court levied countless fines for removing faggots and bundles of firewood from the College wood, and for breaking hedges and fences for the same purpose. The very fact that it had to issue such warnings and penalties repeatedly proves how ineffective the court was in stopping the practice.

Times were changing – slowly by modern standards, and still within the framework of the old world – but changing nonetheless.

7

The Church

Documentary evidence about Gamlingay church in the Middle Ages is mostly dull and unappetising fare, usually reflecting disputes about the church's income. But when dealing with a church we do not need to rely on documents quite so much because the building itself is still there, waiting to reveal at least some of its secrets.

To me, Gamlingay church is both a graceful and a solid-looking church, built with fieldstones rubbed round and smooth by glaciers thousands of years ago, and rough-hewn blocks of carstone; 'fair large and Comely', as the anti- quarian William Cole described it in the eighteenth century. The enormous circular depression left when the carstone was quar- ried saw later service as the village butts, and later still as the village pound. The church is a conglomerate of many

44

different styles and periods. Parts of the building date from the thirteenth century, a bit more from the fourteenth, including the tower, but it was during the religious revival of the fifteenth century that the most delightful part of the church was built – a set of wooden choir-stalls. A wood-carver was employed to embellish the misericords, a sort of perch on the underside of each seat, used by those who were required to stand during the long services. He attacked the unadorned wood with great gusto, and obviously had a lot of fun. The misericords were transformed into a demon's head, an ape, grapes in vine leaves and a crouching man with what looks like the weight of the world on his shoulders. The little handgrips between the seats get similar treatment, becoming an angel, a mitred bishop and a variety of fantastic animals. They are all beautifully carved. The stonemasons, perhaps taking their cue from the anonymous wood-carver, produced equally charming results with their open-jawed gargoyles. My particular favourite is a marvellous dog, lolling on his back and leering at the world through his hind legs. Both wood-carvings and stonework provide an illuminating insight into the fears, obsessions and sense of humour of the medieval mind.

Walter Taylard, steward of Merton and moneyed landowner, recorded his personal wealth and piety for posterity to admire in another corner of the church by paying for the little chapel of St Katherine to be remodelled. Taylard was undeniably proud of his contribution because he mentions it in his will, dated 1464, asking to be buried in the 'chapel of St Katherine newly built by me'. The Taylards, having paid for it, not unnaturally thought they had proprietorial rights. His wife carved the words '*hic est sedes Margarete Taylard*' ('this is the seat of Margaret Taylard') on a pillar next to the chapel. The message is clear enough; how she expected ordinary villagers to understand her Latin is not so obvious. Margaret Taylard outlived her husband by eleven years. In her will she asked to be buried beside her husband in St Katherine's chapel. In common with many of the priesthood and the laity, they had a commemorative brass made, set upon 'a faire marble stone' according to John Layer, who saw it a century and a half later. He also liked the church, describing it as 'a very hanesome faire large church'.

The explosion of 'good works' in the early fifteenth century resulted in the presence of half a dozen priests, both everyday ones and chantry priests, although no specific chantries are recorded. But the work of building a more substantial and ornate church came to an end around the time John Alcock, the Bishop of Ely, visited the parish in 1490 to consecrate a brand-new great bell, a small bell, and two new altars. From the prayer that he ordained should be offered by the faithful on hearing the small bell toll ('God have mercy of John Busshop of Ely that halowede the Altares and Bellys') one might be forgiven for thinking that he was trying to take some of the credit for himself.

What was it like inside a medieval church? It would have been dark, chilly and eerie, with candles flickering in gloomy corners where the light falling through the gaudy stained-glass windows failed to penetrate. There were no seats, or very few until the sixteenth century. Most of the congregation sat on the rush-strewn floor or lounged against the pillars, bored by an interminable service in Latin which few, if any, could understand. This probably accounts for the fact that most of the pillars are covered in an indescribable and often indecipherable mass of graffiti – '*hic est sedes*' and '*mors comparat umbre*' among them. For those who had forgotten their knives there were the wall-paintings to gaze at. What they looked like is a mystery. Lurid biblical scenes such as the Mouth of Hell and the Day of Judgement were popular, but a smudge or two of red ochre is all that survives in Gamlingay church. As for fixtures and fittings, we have some documentary evidence from a book called *Vetus Liber Archidiaconi Eliensis*, dating from about 1278. After telling us that the church pays 30 marks tax, 2s. 4d. for synodal dues, 18d. for procuration and 5s. for Peter's pence, it lists the books belonging to the church. There were two mass-books, two books of antiphons, two books of tropes (verses sung by the choir), two books of anthems, one book of legends (saints' lives and edifying lessons from scripture), a service book and a calendar of saints and benefactors known as a book of obits. Apart from these handwritten and illuminated books the church owned:

3 pairs of vestments with appurtenances
4 surplices
1 rochet (white linen vestment)

4 phials (cruets – small vessels for wine or water)
Chrism cloth (confirmation cloth)
2 altar fronts
8 banners

Over the next century or two small additions or replacements are listed: four chalices, a lamp and a censer by 1303 (we met this censer in Chapter 2, in the bailiffs' accounts when Merton College bought it for the church), three cushions and a new vestment of blue and gold brocade by 1400, but the books and furniture listed in 1278 are representative of the basic requirements of a medieval church.

The church, however, was more than just a place for worship: it was the hub of village social life too. The annual celebration of the local saint's feast-day was held within it, as were church ales, an alcoholic equivalent of a church bazaar, while the holy days of the Church calendar were the villagers' holidays. The church was a sanctuary for criminals on the run, parish strongroom, parish storehouse, parish armoury and frequently did service as a reliable place to conduct business transactions. People thought that promises made within the church were less likely to be broken than those made elsewhere, and perhaps they had a point. For a reference to this custom I beg leave to leap forward to the year 1645 for a moment, and quote from the will of Christopher Mead. When he left some money to his son and asked for payment to be made in 'the south porch of the parish church' he was simply following a long tradition.

Whether in its religious role or in its social role, the church dominated village life in a way that is difficult to imagine now. It was both of the village, and outside it, fulfilling the spiritual needs of the community and providing evidence of the wider world outside the village bounds. It played, and still plays, a central part in the three main ceremonial rites a person passes through: birth, marriage and death. No documentary evidence survives from the Middle Ages for the first two in Gamlingay, although the thirteenth-century baptismal font, with a piece or two of an earlier one incorporated in it, solidly proclaims its part in village life through the centuries.

Death is a different matter. Visible signs of death are everywhere: indented slabs of stone, their brasses long gone, memorial tablets, medieval stone coffin-lids, and, most obvious of all, the churchyard. I do not mean the crosses and gravestones, which date from a later period, but the fact that the churchyard stands 3 or 4 feet higher than the surrounding land. It is, quite simply, full to overflowing with the mouldering bones of long-dead villagers.

At the same time as the revival of the Church was taking place there grew up an organisation whose nearest modern equivalent would be, I suppose, the Friendly Society. The thousands of guilds which sprang up all over the country provided, for the outlay of a penny or two a week, mutual protection against old age, infirmity and poverty. At the same time they enabled the guild member to be sure of a good funeral and that masses would be said on the anniversary of his death (the obit). The guild of the Trinity in Gamlingay was founded in the late fifteenth century and employed its own brotherhood priest, owned a guildhall, a malt-mill, cottages and at least sixty acres of land – all gifts given piecemeal over the years, as the king's commissioners discovered when they confiscated them. The Acts of Parliament suppressing the guilds were passed in 1546, and this is what the guild of the Trinity possessed in terms of domestic equipment at about that date:

2 brasse pottes; one brasse panne; one trevett of Iron; one dosen of pewter platters; 8 disshes; 6 sawsers; 3 towelles.

The whole lot was valued at a pound. Other than this list of utensils used during the annual guild-feast and quoted as much for the appeal of words and phrases like 'trevett' and 'one dosen of pewter platters' as for anything else, there is not much more I can add about the guild of the Trinity. The guildhall was sold and the priest given a pension of 96s. The passing of the guild caused a certain amount of harm and hardship to villagers and brought little benefit – either in terms of money or prestige – to the king.

I want to leave this brief chapter on the church by giving here a few of the bequests in villagers' wills made before the Reformation. They clearly show the place of the church and the guild in the villagers' lives:

1505
Nicholas Ancten alias Malton: 'unto the high awter . . . for myn oblacions and tithes forgoten 10s. . . . the brotherhod of the blissed Trynitie of Gamlyngey shall have an acre of my lond . . .'

1522
William Fox: 'To the mayntenyns of the Torches 3s. 4d.' . . .

'I bequeth to the Paynting of Saint Katerin in Gamlingay 3s. 4d.'

1526
Richard Berry: Executors to 'by a laten Candilstick with 5 burnruches to be set befor the trinitie', and son to 'fynd Tapure burnyng before the Trinite . . . every holidaie and fridaie the tyme of Devyn service . . .'

1532
Thomas Ancten alias Malton: Gives 'to the Church of Gamlingay too silver candellsticks price of tenne pounds.'

'4d. yerely or wex of the value of 4d. to the mayntennance of the said light or tapers that comonly stande aboute the herse . . .'

'40s. spente eqaly upon the moost necessary uses of the bretherhede in Gamlingaye in buylding of the churche house and the amendement of the highe wayes . . .'

1538
John Nicholas: 'to the bretherred of the blessed trinitie 2s.'

1543
Thomas Huckle: 'to the rale lyght 4d.'

1544
Elizabeth Whiting: 'towards the maintennance of the sepulcre lyght 2 powndes of wex.'

1544
William Coliche: 'to the plowelyght 2 busshells Barly.'

1546
Joan Golde: 'to Robert, guylde prist of gamlyngay, a sylver spone.'

1546
John Fylbarne: 'to the hy auter a buschell of barley.' . . .

'to the bells a buschell of barley.'

8

Court Rolls

From the 1450s onwards England was wracked by civil war – the Wars of the Roses that every school-child learns about – and the country was left to fend for itself. It is difficult to escape the conclusion that what the common people did with their new-found freedom was to abuse it. The art of selfishness became highly developed. To a large extent the days of truly communal agriculture were over, and with them went the means for the less well-off to claw some kind of independent living from the soil. Some people prospered under these new conditions. Low rents and the ability to farm more productively by combining strips of land into compact blocks enabled these future yeomen to become wealthy farmers and landowners. Many who were less fortunate slid to the bottom of the heap to become landless labourers, wherein lay the seeds of the vagabond problem which was to plague successive centuries.

A very few climbed a good deal further. One such was William Purchase. He was born in Gamlingay in about 1440, the son of an alewife. From comparative poverty he became a rich mercer in London, rising eventually to become Mayor of London in 1497/8. When he died in 1503 he was the Tudor equivalent of a millionaire.

But that story is outside the scope of this book. In Gamlingay the concern with self-interest, coupled with the violent nature of some of the men who were fighting their way out of the old villein class, is reflected in the manor court rolls of the period. I shall return to those rolls now to carry the story of the village through to the end of the fifteenth century. They run virtually continuously from 1461 until 1499, with four rolls surviving from the early sixteenth century (1501, 1508, 1509 and 1510/11), and the contents of this chapter are based on them.

We have seen the beginnings of a selfish outlook earlier in the century when families like the Fishers dominated the court's activities, but by the end of the century the Fishers were respectable folk, established members of the village hierarchy. Paradoxically they had risen to a position where they now sat in judgement on those people trying to emulate them. I should imagine that they were suitably indignant at the way some went about it – there are few as unforgiving as a reformed sinner.

Might was right, as it usually is. The only way to settle an argument, seemingly, was to resort to blows. This selection of cases heard by the court illustrates what I mean. I only wish I could provide some background information to them.

John Warde, 'plowghwrite', assaulted William Ongear with a stick called a 'lever' worth a halfpenny and drew his blood, contrary to the king's peace. Fined 4d.

Thomas Taylor, fined 6d., assaulted Northerne Johnson, fined 2d., with a stick and drew his blood.

Ralph Weyber assaulted Robert [blank] with a 'hanger' [ie a pothanger]. Fined 2d.

The same Robert assaulted the said Ralph and struck him with a jar, throwing it at his head.

Philip Thesler assaulted William Paule, firing an arrow at him. Fined 4d.

Robert Stabelar assaulted the aforesaid Philip Thesler, throwing a 'hanger' at him. Fined 2d.

Walter Aythorppe, fined 2d., and William Paule assaulted Thomas Barber with two weapons in their hands.

John Birt assaulted Agnes Wache and struck her in the face with his hand. Fined 6d.

Robert Fuller assaulted Thomas Holme's servant by throwing a stone at him and drew his blood. Fined 6d.

At times the air must have been thick with flying arrows, stones, pothangers and the like. It seems reminiscent of nothing so much as a lot of rowdy children in the school playground. In a way these fifteenth-century villagers *were* like school-children, newly released from the restrictions of the past and yet to learn that freedom carries its own responsibilities. Many of the incidents can be put down to the general atmosphere of lawlessness prevailing at the time, and none are particularly serious. The village constables (there were normally two) were supposed to deal with such outbreaks of — to be charitable — boisterous ill-feeling, but with one half of the village endlessly feuding with the other half it was an impossible task. It was also a thankless one, as William Burley, the constable, discovered.

Edward Langton seems to have planned the ambush of Thomas Russell quite cold-bloodedly, and although I am only guessing there may have been an element of inter-manorial dispute behind the attack. Langton farmed the Sawtry estate. Whatever the reason, it is clear that Langton was taking no chances. As Russell was making his way to the manor court on the morning of Tuesday 8 May 1492 — five months before Columbus discovered America — he was set upon by Langton and a band of his servants armed with 'six sticks and knives and an unlawful bandog'. They

assaulted Thomas Russhell within the bounds and limits of this lordship, and then and there beat him and wounded him, badly cutting him and drawing his blood contrary to the king's peace.

'Bandog' implies some sort of hunting dog, probably a mastiff. If 'bounds and limits of this lordship' means that the assault took place within the manorial gates, which I think it does, then Langton must have felt really sure of himself.

The constable, William Burley, probably witnessed the assault. He was one of the jurors and would have been at the court early to be sworn in. I doubt very much if he lifted a finger to protect Russell (it would have been a brave man who did) but the rest of the court, despite their own lack of action, obviously felt that Burley should have done something. The clerk has written in the margin beside the record of this case that 'John Fox is elected constable instead of William Burley and is sworn'. Possibly it was easier for the court to blame the constable than to examine their own consciences. Poor William Burley! I feel sorry for him, especially considering the stew his son was to get into some forty years later when faced with much the same predicament.

Langton, meanwhile, was fined the hefty sum of 5s. and his servants 20d., although whether his servants were fined individually or collectively I cannot say. These fascinating yet frustrating documents seldom tell the whole story. I am pretty sure the fines were not paid – at least there seems to be no record of them being paid – but there was little the court could do about it.

Much of the violence could be blamed on the influence of the alcohol served in the village alehouses. There were as many as ever: nine alewives were fined in 1487 and seven in 1495 for example. But now some establishments had developed into something a little closer to the modern-day public house. Three, indeed, had acquired names. They had always had names of course: 'Mother Basse's place' or 'Spede's house' or something similar; but from now on one hears of 'the Cock' in Church Street, 'the Falcon' at the crossroads, and 'the Swan'. The Cock, first noted in a rental dating from 1470/71, is still going strong today in a later Elizabethan house on the same site. I am intrigued by the fact that a rental from around 1490 mentions the 'signum de le cokke' and the 'signum de le Swan'. These are early references to inn-signs, which did not become fashionable for another 200 years. The owners of the Cock and the Swan must have been trendsetters. The owner of the Falcon was none other than William Burley, erstwhile constable. The Falcon was in fact a converted farmhouse known during most of the Middle Ages as 'Whitehall'.

William Gosson was an innkeeper who believed in providing entertainment for his customers, as this next quotation illustrates:

1475
William Gosson, innkeeper, aided by various people played unlawful games and sports, namely football, tennis and tables, on feast-days and other illegal times. Fined 6d.

A little explanation is necessary. 'Tables', originally a Roman board-

William Gosson and friend playing tables.

game, resembled backgammon, using dice and counters which the players moved around the board. It was much in vogue with the upper classes throughout the Middle Ages. Tennis was the 'real' variety, but since this requires courts and facilities that I am certain did not exist in the Gamlingay of 1475 it is likely that William Gosson's tennis was pretty poor stuff. Football bore little resemblance to the present game. It was played by hordes of people and was often brutal and dangerous and was frequently banned by the authorities (or perhaps there *is* some similarity with modern football).

Another illegal way of enjoying oneself (though most of these activities were illegal), and a useful way of adding to the family's fare, was to indulge in a spot of poaching, although half the 'sport', then as now, was in running the risk of capture. A couple of examples amongst many will do. William Rede was fined fourpence in 1471 for taking rabbits and hares 'with greyhounds and other animals', while in 1489 the court heard that Richard Frances, Thomas Derlyng, William Burley and Richard Aythorpe were 'common poachers who do not hold land and tenements worth more than 40s. and they own greyhounds and hunt by scent. Fined 2d. each'. I must hastily point out that William Burley was not the village constable at the time. Note the financial restrictions on keeping greyhounds and hunting: one either had to own property worth 40s. a year for taxation purposes or goods worth £5 in order to indulge man's innate instinct to hunt. This ensured, as it was meant to, that taking game remained 'hunting' for the well-to-do and 'poaching' for everybody else.

Those people with a keen interest in their neighbours' business could find many opportunities to amuse themselves. With no street lighting, easy access to the village tofts and crofts and paper-thin wattle walls it was child's play to spend the long winter evenings listening in to other villagers' private conversations. All the stranger, then, that this is the only case of its kind in the court records:

1461
The jury say that Thomas Jervis is a common 'evisdropper', hiding at night below the tenants' houses. He listens to what the tenants say in their houses and repeats it all in suspect speech contrary to the law of the land. Fined 6d.

And what was Thomas Jervis's wife doing while her husband was out at night gathering gossip? She had found her own way of passing the time:

Rose his wife furtively took 'Otemele and flowir' from William Baldry's goods after the feast of the Nativity last. Fined 6d.

I have said before that theft was a much rarer occurrence in the medieval village than one might have imagined, and, for what they are worth, here are the only other cases from this period:

1463
Isabella Sprottele stole corn from the tenant's sheaves during last harvest. Fined 6d.

1494
John Wolff unjustly took a calfskin and a piece of clout-leather from an unknown man. Fined 12d.

The situation regarding the disrepair of village houses seems to have got progressively worse. One example: the court instructed John and Robert Warde in 1487 to 'repair their tenements sufficiently in all things before Michaelmas'. This was greeted with inactivity. The order was repeated in 1490, when it was added that the timber and thatch needed repair. The Wardes were given until the following Easter to make it good on pain of a fine of 10s. Four years later the

instructions were repeated. Yet again they were ignored. The following year the court ordered them to make good the wood, thatch and
plaster of the tenements and other buildings in their possession, adding
that if they would not carry out the work themselves then the bailiff
would have to do it. Nothing was done, of course, and the order was
repeated in 1496. The following court increased the penalty to 20s.,
dropped the idea of the bailiff doing the work, then quietly let the case
slip from the records *nine years* after first raising it.

Amidst the stony indifference of people like the Wardes and others
who were, absurdly, sitting in judgement on themselves, the early
Tudor village was falling to pieces. Barns and houses were coming to
the end of their useful lives and nobody was prepared to do anything
about it. They would sit happily on the jury and piously order other
people (and themselves) to make the necessary repairs, but immediately the court was finished they would adjourn to the nearest alehouse
and promptly forget all about it.

As far back as 1451 the court had listed many defects around Merton
manor. Among other things, the kiln-house was defective in two bays,
the stables were defective in plaster and woodwork, the sheep-cote was
in bad repair, the hog's cote 'totally decayed' and the dovecote 'has
windows broken in many places by the wind'. They suggested that the
new tenant – William Newton – should make the repairs. Whether
he did or not is a question I cannot answer. By 1491 even the room
in which the jury sat was tumbling down and well-nigh derelict. An
inventory was taken that year when Thomas Bird took over the lease
of the manor farm. Compared to the earlier ones this inventory is brief
in the extreme. There was not, in fact, much to write about: £10's
worth of stock, some cereals, harnesses, harrows, 'dong fork' and
similar small pieces of husbandry hardware, but, significantly, only
one plough. The scribe also noted:

2 table bords.
One payre of trestills.
3 formes.
4 bedbords.
A posnet of a potell [iron pot with a capacity of half a gallon].
A spitte.

This list paints a fine picture of neglect: a trestle table, three forms, four bedboards, the only cooking utensils being a spit and an iron pot. And that is all! The 'manor house' was more like a hovel.

This situation did not exactly inspire a respect for authority in the rest of the population. And when the repairs or rebuilding simply *had* to be done, what happened when building materials were required?

1486
Each person who has made lime in the king's highway for their houses shall make adequate repair on pain of 3s. 4d. before Pentecost next.

Most people considered the road that ran past their house and yard to be their own personal property, and thought nothing of burning lime on it, digging holes in it and removing sand from it. Some folk went to the opposite extreme and left obstructions on it:

1485
Thomas Jenkyn fined 3s. 4d. for placing stones and sand in the king's highway . . .

Jenkyn was almost certainly rebuilding his house. What could be more natural than to block the road with his building materials? Also 'natural' was the obstruction noted in 1487 when John Cler was ordered to 'carry his dung from the king's highway to his gate on pain of 12d.'.

The court spent much of its time during this period repeatedly issuing regulations concerning the government of parish resources. None of the following would have been necessary 200 years before; mutual dependence and common sense would have seen to that.

Nobody shall put or pasture his sheep or horses in 'le litilfenne' from the feast of the Annunciation of the Blessed Virgin Mary until Michaelmas on pain of 6s. 8d.

The lord and all free tenants of this manor who are copyholders shall clean that part of 'le comon brok' where it abuts on their land . . . pain of 6s. 8d.

Ordered that no baker or alewife cut down 'lez Bromes' or 'hethe' on the common except one cartload a year on pain of 6s. 8d.

Nobody shall keep his sheep or pigs by themselves, but shall put them in 'le Flok', on pain of 3s. 4d.

The tenants who so conscientiously repeated these sensible rules and regulations were the same ones who broke them, the same ones who were fined and the same ones who did not pay. But that situation was about to change. As so often happens in history the moment produced the man, and when Henry Tudor defeated Richard III at Bosworth Field on 22 August 1485, the country had found the leader it so badly needed. Although the date is just a convenience, 1485 saw the end of the Middle Ages at hand. It was not quite as dramatic as that, of course. John Warde did not wake up on the morning of August 23 and say to himself, 'the Middle Ages are over – I'd better mend the roof'. The transformation from 'medieval' to 'Tudor' took time. But the village was changing, slowly but surely, and it would be wrong to leave this period without saying a word or two about the two buildings that did get rebuilt, and which still ornament the village today.

Merton College, as we have seen, owned the rectory, which stood slightly to the east of the church, Whitehall, a farm which stood at the crossroads, and Merton Manor Farm. Between 1475 and 1491 all three were leased to an energetic tenant called Thomas Bird. He first leased Whitehall, made some money, then leased the rectory. This was probably falling down when Bird took it over because he built a new timber-framed rectory, with a magnificent open hall and a cross-wing at the south end. The stains left by the smoke as it tried to find its way

Merton Manor Farm as it is today

from the hearth in the hall out through the louvre in the roof are still plainly visible today. With some later additions and much recent restoration the rectory is second only to Merton Manor Farm as the finest building in the village. Thomas Bird built that too, as he moved onwards and upwards and grew in wealth. When he took it over in 1491 it was all but uninhabitable, as the inventory I have just quoted shows. Like the rectory, the new manor farm was built in solid yeomanly style with an open hall and a cross-wing, but on a larger scale. Here, too, later building and modern restoration have worked wonders and produced a splendid house.

9

Moche Busynes: The Slade Affair

It was a Sunday in early March 1532. One of those feuds which always seemed to be simmering just beneath the outwardly calm surface of the village was about to explode into a brief but bitterly violent life. Although the eruption only lasted a few hours it threw up enough incident to keep those involved in anecdotes for the rest of their lives.

In telling this tale I am relying on sworn statements relating to two cases heard by the Court of Star Chamber in London. All the documents are now in the Public Record Office. The chief characters in this little drama were as follows:

Edward Slade: a wealthy farmer of Avenel's manor, although there is only indirect evidence for this. Rather a shadowy figure until this court case throws him into sharp relief.

John Burley: constable. Son of William Burley, the unfortunate constable we met previously. Like his father, he kept the Falcon alehouse.

Thomas Chicheley: esquire, Justice of the Peace, owner of a large estate at Wimpole. Came from a well-to-do merchant family, which was just about the only really dominant family in Cambridgeshire at the time. Tended to be rather high-handed in dishing out justice.

To say Edward Slade was unpopular with his neighbours is an under-statement. If his fellow villagers are to be believed, Slade was little better than a bandit. They claimed that he stole a field of wheat from Widow Goores and two crops of peas from John Basse, that he 'mayhemmed' Richard Clark, killed several people's pigs, and when Mistress Barker tried to save her pig from his clutches it was said that he clouted her across the hand with a mole-spade so hard that she was unable to move it 'soo wele as she myght before'. Thomas Ratford lost a bullock, one 'Trollop' lost his hay when Slade broke open a barn door and threw the contents in the yard, and the village constable, John Burley, was set upon when he tried to prevent Slade and his cronies stealing the tithes from the tithe barn. Slade took a flock of sheep belonging to William Malden and held it ransom for 20s., and his servants turned the corn out of John Hedding's cart. Thomas Huckle claimed that most of the village went 'dayly in daynger of ther bodyes' because of Edward Slade. He was a black-hearted fellow – if you believe it all.

The spark which ignited the pent-up feeling was yet another assault, perpetrated on John Basse by one of Slade's servants, who was put up to it by his master. It might have remained just another grudge to add to the long list of grudges against Edward Slade but for one crucial difference: Basse asked the constable to arrest Slade and obtain sureties that he and his servant Malpas would keep the peace. Perhaps John Burley thought that this was the chance to take revenge on Slade. Perhaps he believed it was an opportunity to make amends for his father William Burley's dismissal, forty years before. Perhaps he felt safer surrounded by his fellow villagers, few of whom were well-disposed to Slade. Whatever the reasoning, John Burley made a big mistake in choosing to arrest Slade while he was hearing mass in the church. He obviously had not learned from the experience of the king's bailiff who had tried to arrest Slade in the church two years before. On that occasion Slade's servants had 'kept the chapell dore shett' until Slade had made his escape.

From this point on there are twenty-three different accounts, in varying degrees of detail, to choose from, which only goes to show that 'truth' is a highly subjective matter. After reading them all this is my opinion of what happened.

Slade was kneeling in the chapel of St Katherine when Burley entered the church and attempted the arrest. The words Burley used are not recorded; nor is the answer given by Slade. Who hit whom first is a matter of dispute. Slade said forcibly that if anyone laid hands on him then he would fight back. There was some pushing and shoving, then a punch was thrown. Burley was cuffed on the ear and then hit in the mouth so that 'he did spett blood', before Slade grabbed a staff and started hitting the constable with it. He then pulled out his wood-knife, and Burley thumped him 'on the Ere with his ffyst'. Before a real brawl could develop the two protagonists were pulled apart and Slade made his way from the church and went home. The rest of the congregation, no doubt enjoying the fight, began excitedly discussing it and there was 'moche busynes, some spake of the oon parte and some on the other' as William Myddelton so vividly testified.

The scene now shifts outside the church. The constable, licking his wounds and smoothing down the ruffled feathers of authority, was approached by Slade's friend John Bridges, who offered to put up surety for his friend. This Burley refused, claiming that he had no authority to accept.

Unfortunately this left John Burley in something of a quandary. A failed arrest was liable to make his position in the village difficult, yet bloodshed was the likely consequence of trying to arrest Slade on home ground. At the same time, he was responsible for law and order in the parish. If he had decided to drop the matter the incident would in all probability have been forgotten and Burley would only have had a bruise or two and a red face to worry about. But injured pride and the memory of his father's failure were obviously foremost in his thoughts, so he took the only other course open to him and sent to Thomas Chicheley, esquire and Justice of the Peace, for help.

Chicheley was obviously in no hurry to spoil his Sunday rest by riding out from Wimpole to sort out the tiresome problems of one of his constables. Instead, he despatched a couple of his men to ascertain the facts of the matter, and it was only when they failed to return in good time (probably confused by the conflicting stories) that he wearily pulled on his boots, mounted his horse, called four of his men to join him and set off for Gamlingay.

The first thing he did on arrival was to head for The Cock, where he was able to quench his thirst while listening to the constable's tale of woe. After calling for most of the men of the village to join him, Chicheley sent two friends of Slade, John Bridges and Stephen Butler, to Slade to request the pleasure of his company. 'Sent' is perhaps not the right word. They were bullied and cajoled into going with the threat that they would end up in Cambridge Castle if they did not do as they were told. Slade's answer was predictable: he refused. Chicheley decided to go home and make the most of what was left of his Sunday, but as he was leaving the villagers came to him, crying that if he went then they were going with him, 'for they sayd they knewe well murdre was lyke to ensue, and manslawter, without his helpe'. At least, that was how Thomas Chicheley justified what happened next.

Moved by the appeal, he sent the two reluctant messengers back to Slade, this time to say that should Slade refuse to come to him as ordered he would take him as a rebel, and that he would 'pulle the tyles over his hede', a phrase which sounds much more like the authentic Chicheley than the reluctant hero we have seen so far.

The two wretched messengers returned, unable to find Slade. Someone claimed to have seen him going into his house with 'bowe and arrowes in his hand'. On hearing this Chicheley's patience snapped. Taking Bridges, Butler, Burley and the rest of the village men armed with 'swords and buklers and some byllis' Chicheley led his motley army down Church Street and round to Slade's house, which lay on the outskirts of the village. I should think that most of the men were glad of the chance to settle some old scores.

The sight of the mob bearing down on him obviously frightened Slade, who, whatever else he might have been, was no coward. In his own words, he was 'in grete feer and dout of his lyfe' when he saw Chicheley and his band in 'suche angre and fury'. He hastily ordered the doors to be shut, and, taking a bow and some arrows, rushed to an upstairs window overlooking the yard. One of his servants also grabbed a bow and ran to a window.

Chicheley, never one to spurn action, with an angry mob at his back and a refractory man in front, told his men to pull down the 'pales standyng abowght the house', and the crowd surged forward into the courtyard. Slade responded by loosing a few arrows in their direction, and his servant did likewise. As William College put it, 'the master as the man shott arrowes out at the wyndowes . . . and struke Chicheley his servant throwe the knee . . .'. Slade was to claim rather weakly that he only fired one arrow without a head on it, thereby putting the blame for the injury squarely on the shoulders of his own servant.

Having lost his patience half an hour before, Chicheley now lost his temper. He bawled 'break down the doors', or something like it, because everyone who was there agrees that some of the mob pulled up 'a gret post in ther hands and ran at the halle doore'. This improvised battering-ram quickly smashed a way in to the house, but how was Chicheley to get the two offenders out of their respective rooms? Once again, he opted for action rather than words. He shouted 'down with the doores', and started 'crying for Gune powder, and sayd they wold burne Slade out of the house'. In the excitement that followed doors were 'brake opyn' and both Slade and the mysterious servant were brought before Chicheley, Slade claiming that it was done with 'grete vyolence' and that he was dragged from his chamber by the mob, 'some by the leggs and some by the armes'. Everyone else says that he was persuaded to come out by John Bridges and Stephen Butler, his friends.

Despite claims to the contrary, it is quite clear that once in Chicheley's hands the two prisoners were roughly treated and dragged off with very little ceremony up Church Street to the village stocks. Stephen Butler adds some picturesque details of the manner in which Slade in particular was conveyed:

as soone as Chicheley hadde Slade he causyd hym mayntenant to be ledde to the stokks and throwe a myre by the waye, and ther kept hym fast lokkyd . . .

Slade's mud-spattered state was not improved by the weather of that Sunday in March. In a delightful phrase which succeeds in rolling back the centuries, William Myddelton tells us 'it rayned a lytyll, *soft pase*'.

Securely locked up, the troublesome pair were left in the drizzle to cool off for an hour or two. Slade said later that while he was being dragged (in John Bridges's words) 'in cruell manner throwe the myre', a little over £7 was stolen from his house. Were I uncharitable I should suggest it was buying round after round of ale for his conquerors, by now safely out of the rain and back in the warm and convivial atmosphere of The Cock. After the two prisoners had stewed for a while they were put on a horse and sent with an escort towards Cambridge Castle. They reached Caxton that evening, 'beyng 3 myles thense', and lodged there for the night. And then?

... the next mornyng they brought hym befor Mr Sutton, beyng Justice of the Peace, wher he found suertes and so was set at large.

Thus Edward Slade, battered, bruised, muddied and no doubt as defiant as ever, went home, to nourish and cultivate his hatred of the men who had bested him.

The case Slade brought against Burley, Chicheley and the rest in the Court of Star Chamber was the result of that hatred. We are not told the outcome of the case, which is unfortunate, to say the least. You can feel the burning indignation of Slade, Butler and Bridges at the rough handling they received. You can see the angelic expressions on the defendants' faces as they denied the allegations to a man. You can follow the action through all its stages, making due allowance for bias and contradictions in the evidence, but, maddeningly, the result of the case remains a mystery. Nevertheless, I think it is safe to say Slade lost – eventually. Against him were the sworn testimonies of seventeen respectable men, including a Justice of the Peace and a constable. For him were a few friends willing to swear to his heavy-handed treatment but unwilling to swear that the arrest was unjustified. What happened to Edward Slade was probably seen by the court as a rough-and-ready form of justice.

The case dragged on and on until John Burley and the others were so fed up with it that they brought a retaliatory action against Slade. I do not know the result of that case either, but I am fairly sure that Slade left the village soon afterwards. He does not appear in any village record after 1532. Being a wealthy man he must have made a will, but I have not found one. After these two court cases Edward Slade simply disappears.

Finally, there is further amusement to be found in the evidence given by those who did not play a large part in the day's events. Where, for

instance, was John Basse, who began the whole affair by asking the constable to arrest Slade? The poor man was ill:

Sayeth as to all the residew of the Articles he can little depose, for somoche as he was not present, but was at home in his own howse, *being very evyll at ease and sickely*. And more he doth not know but by report.

A likely story. He was well out of the way because he knew trouble was afoot. Somewhat surprisingly, Thomas St George, owner of Avenel's manor and, if my guesswork is correct, Slade's landlord, was indicted too. His defence was that he 'dwellyth in another parysshe dystannt from the sayd parysshe of Gamlinga a myle or more callyd Hatle, beyng at his awn parysshe churche so that he sawe no parte of any demeanour'; and besides, said Thomas St George, he too was 'acrasyd of a Surfett the day menconned'. There was a lot of it about.

The perfect antithesis to the violence and anger is the testimony of gentle Thomas Pekket, the parish priest, and an old man of fifty-eight.

He, it seems, was like the three wise monkeys: he saw nothing, heard nothing, and was saying nothing:

afor the sayd arrest and afor any suche busynes this deponent hadde sayd masse and was gone in visitacon so that he can not depose in it.

Mr Chicheley came to the town when this deponent was at evynsong, and there this deponent contynuyd tyll they hadde arrestyd Slade and can not depose in the mater further, for he was not among them, nor dyd see any of the demeanour . . .

Perhaps, on reflection, his was the sanest course of all.

10

The Uncertain Hour of Death

Unless one is very lucky and can draw upon such documents as the court case in the previous chapter, virtually the only way one can get any idea of the lives and characters of village people before the modern era is through their wills. These are, to my mind, the most interesting and personal of all documents to read 'in the flesh'. Most of those made by Gamlingay men and women are kept, along with thousands of others, in the vast collection belonging to the University Library in Cambridge, where they are available for inspection. A few more are in the Public Record Office in London. I have copies of 149 Gamlingay wills from the period 1500 to 1650, and of those, the thirty-six covering the first half-century or so of that period will concern us here.

The majority of those wills bound in large leather volumes in the University Library and all those kept in the Public Record Office are copies of original wills. On rare occasions an original will turns up, written at the testator's bedside, which with their crossings-out and changes of mind are even more interesting. Wills were normally written in English, in an ink which has remained remarkably fresh and in the 'secretary' script of the period.

All wills start with a preamble, and, since we have already met him in the last chapter, I shall use that of John Basse to give the general idea:

In the name of God amen, The 11th daye of may the yere of owre lorde God 1534 I John Basse the elder of Gamlingay in the diocess of Ely, beyng hole of mynd and of perfytte remembrance, feryng the incerten houre of dethe, make and orden thys my testament and last wyll in maner and forme folowyng:

Strictly speaking, a will should dispose of real estate and a testament should cover the distribution of personal belongings, but few people bothered with such fine distinctions. Of course, the particular moment when a person set down his last will and testament depended very much upon the individual. Some were written what the testator obviously hoped would be many years before the 'incerten houre of dethe' – or as John Silbarn put it at greater length in 1546: 'nothinge is so sure as deathe and nothynge so uncertaine to man as the owre of deathe'. Others were made at the last possible moment, with the testator lying on his deathbed. Those people who did leave it until the last moment before making a will occasionally mention their illness in it, in the way sick people often have of wanting to discuss their ailments. William Lawe began his will in 1550 by reporting that he was 'by the visitacon of God sykke in bodye', while Elizabeth Whiting, six years earlier, despite being 'sik in my body' was well enough to give thanks for being of 'perfect mynde and memorie, lawde and prayse be to allmyghty God'. Thomas Huckle in 1543 was more concerned that his wife might 'dye upon this syknes' than with the fact that he himself was close to death.

After the preamble the testator made his first bequest. This is typical of most, from John Nicholas in 1538:

I bequeath my sowle to God allmyghtie, to our blessid ladie saynt marie and to all the hollie companie of hevyn, and my bodie to buryed within the parishe churche yarde of gamlyngay.

At first sight this seems to be a piously expressed, deeply-felt religious sentiment, and no doubt it often was, but reading twenty or thirty wills with almost the same wording in each, it soon becomes clear that it was simply a matter of form. So, too, were those bequests to the church quoted earlier – the payments for 'tithes negligently forgotten' and so on. They were part of the custom which said some portion of an estate should go to the parish church.

Sometimes the place of burial was specified more exactly than just 'in the churchyard'. Thomas Bird, the man who built the rectory and Merton Manor Farm, asked to be buried 'beside the crosse there on the South side' in 1505 and Robert Barford (1546) wanted to be laid to rest 'besyde my father and my mother of the northe syde'. William Malden, in his will dated 1550, decreed that his body be 'buryed in the churche porche of the sowght syde', a resting place half way between the common herd heaped together in the churchyard and the upper ranks of society buried within the church itself, a station that presumably he thought he occupied in life as well as in death. Richard Clark, the farmer of Merton manor, was one of those wealthy enough to specify burial within the main body of the church at his death in 1551, asking that it be 'in the mydell allye'.

When the testator had finished with these formalities there was that medieval obsession, 'the health of my soul', to consider. This worry was often assuaged by a payment to the parish priest or priests for a mass to be sung each year on the anniversary of the testator's demise. Thousands of priests made a comfortable living this way. John Basse showed typical care in providing for the well-being of his soul by asking William Burley, a friar of the Augustinian order in Cambridge, to sing thirty masses for his soul. Not that John Basse was concerned only with his own soul; some money he gave the guild of the Trinity was to be used to pray for:

my soull, the soull of Amy my wyff, the soull of John Bass my father and also hys wyff, the soull of Henry Bass my grandfather and his wyff and all chrysten souls.

This is a useful start for anyone trying to construct the Basse family tree. John Basse showed a foresight that few of us are blessed with or that any of his fellow villagers possessed (witness his timely confinement, 'evyll at ease and sickely', during the Chicheley-Slade rumpus) and this well-developed sense of caution is displayed in his gift of 8s. to the parish guild. He added the proviso that the money would go to the church and parish instead if:

the forseyd guyld be not maynteined, and that a priest do not contynew in service ther to synge for the brethren and systren, as doth nowe at thys present tyme and season . . .

This wariness was no doubt brought about by Henry VIII's break with Rome, but it was to be more than a decade before Basse's fears were justified and the parish guilds suppressed.

Concern for the soul is a recurring theme in the wills. Thomas Ancten in 1532 left provision for the churchwardens to receive eight cows in order to keep a yearly obit for himself and his wife and 'all our good friends'. The cows were then let out to poor men for 1s. a year, but the poor of the parish were often beneficiaries in a more direct way. Frequently such bequests were small, partly, I suppose, because the guild of the Trinity did its bit to help the poor and aged; partly, too, because the problem of poverty was not so acute as it was to become later in the century. Here are a couple of examples:

Elizabeth Whiting: 'to distribute amongst the pore folks in Gamlingay one Come of malte.'

Robert Barford: 'I gyve to the poore folke to be delte amonge them 3s. at my buryall day.'

Gifts to the poor could also become merely a matter of form, but genuine philanthropic feeling was often the motive. Thomas Ancten provides a good example of what I mean. He requested that during Lent for six years after his death his executors should give to the poor:

oon barrell of White herynge and oon kade of Red herring, the same to be delte every Fryday, to eche of the pour people two White herryngs and oon Red . . .

His executors must have been thrilled to bits to be given such a task. A cade was a barrel of herrings containing about 700 fish (red herrings were smoked and white herrings pickled in brine, incidentally). If every poor person received three fish there were either an awful lot of poor in the parish – 700 or so by my reckoning – or Ancten was using the word 'poor' in a spiritual sense to include all the villagers. But then, I suppose a man who could afford to leave two silver candlesticks worth the enormous sum of £10 to the church might easily look upon the rest of the parish as 'poor'.

There are many bequests in the wills which reflect a perennial problem common to rich and poor alike: the appalling state of the roads and bridges. The roads, which were everybody's dumping ground and quarry when it was convenient, became someone else's problem when they needed repair. In winter they were virtually impassable rivers of mud and dung, and in summer choking, deeply-rutted dustbowls. Small wonder that Edward Slade took such exception to being dragged through the streets on a wet March day, or that one often comes across bequests like these two, taken from the will made in 1505 by Thomas Ancten's sixty-two-year-old father Nicholas Ancten.

I geve unto a lane callid Pevely lane to amend the high wey – 3s. 4d.

Likewise unto another wey callid Spitell lane – 3s. 4d.

Small bequests like that probably paid for a load or two of stones to be tipped into the more dangerous potholes, but they would never solve the problem. Similarly, the bridges over the brook were usually in a bad state of repair. Money was only spent on them when they were in immediate danger of falling down, or had actually crashed into the muddy water beneath. Once again, it was left to individuals to help out, and once again, it is to the Anctens (Thomas this time) that I turn for an illustration. Concern for the village and its inhabitants seems to have been an Ancten trait:

to the reparacon of the bridge called mille bridge and mending the high way in Gamlingay – 13s. 4d.

But the real interest in these wills lies in the more personal details they contain. Most of the people who made wills were men, at least in the first half of the sixteenth century, and this tends to give rather a one-sided view of life. The reason so few women made wills was that the husband had usually settled all the financial arrangements in his will for a period long after his wife's lifetime. A wife who died before her husband had no need to make a will because any property she owned at her marriage had become her husband's. The first concern of most married men, after they had provided for the well-being of their soul, was with the welfare of their wife and children.

It was customary for a woman who brought her own possessions with her when she was wed to be given them back in her husband's will, although legally they belonged to him. John Nicholas represented the view of many men when he referred to these domestic goods as 'trasshe of howsolde'. This clause in Richard Clark's will is similar to many, although it contains a bonus his wife probably did not expect:

I bequeathe to my wyff all suche goodes and cattale [chattels] as she had when I fyrst maryed her, or to the number and valew of them, and £5 besydes . . .

Hidden behind these arrangements for returning a wife's 'portion' to her lies a tangle of economic bargains entered into at the time of marriage. To a man like Richard Clark and many like him, marriage was primarily a business transaction, little concerned with mutual affection. Clark's widow had nothing to worry about financially, with a husband rich enough to leave three houses, cash bequests of about £160, a hundred sheep and much else besides. She herself was catered for in admirable fashion, receiving:

my howse for her to dwell in that joynes next to the parsonage, with the close and 10 acres Lande, untyll Clement Bygrave be 20 yeres of age, yf she lyve so longeth . . .

As a well-endowed widow (in the material sense) with no children, she would not have remained on the marriage market for long. However, most less well-off men had to wrack their brains in order to provide for their widow and children, usually coming up with complicated plans full of 'if-this-should-happen' and 'if-it-happens-that . . .'. In most cases their plans were almost certainly ignored, or failed to take all possible likelihoods into consideration, or were so confused in their meaning that the lawyers must have rubbed their hands with glee and dreamed of extortionate fees and lengthy court cases.

John Burley solved the problem simply enough when he made his will in 1545 by leaving to his wife Margaret 'my house that I nowe dwell in called the Fawcon for terme of her lyffe'. In a rather more long-winded way Thomas Ratford, owner of The Cock, gave his wife all 'Inward Stuff perteynyng to howsold' with instructions to 'bake and brue and Sell other vyttells to her awne use and profytt'. Their son Robert was given joint ownership of the Cock with his mother until she died, and was told in no uncertain terms 'to have nothyng to do with all'. Nicholas Ancten gets a good mark from me for giving his wife 'free dwelling' in his house for the rest of her life, and an extra one for defining it so pleasantly:

'she to have the houses and gardyn plott which I dwell in myselfe, and so to have free goyng and comyng therto, both for hirself and hir frendes.'

Nicholas Ancten was obviously a loving, caring husband. He provided for his beloved Alice still further by telling his son Thomas to pay her 13s. 4d. a year, neglect of which would cost him his father's property, as well as ordering him to till and compost five acres of land out of his own pocket, give her some 'pasteryng and Wynter pastering' for a cow, and take her a load of firewood each year. The Anctens were a rather special family, I think.

The good Nicholas apart, many men attached conditions to these bequests to their wives. Richard Berry in 1526, for instance, gave his wife all his land and in the same breath warned her to 'mak no wast apon the saym'. Gifts like this were normally for 'the terme of her lyfe' only, the husband usually providing for the bequest to revert to his heir or another of his children when she died. A frequent condition attached to these bequests concerns the possibility of a widow's remarriage. However 'sick in body' the husband happened to be, he nearly always had at least half his mind on this likelihood. One might suppose it stemmed from jealousy, but knowing how many men of this will-making class had contracted loveless marriages of convenience this does not seem a very likely explanation. To my mind, the will of an admittedly rather neurotic man called William Whiting who died in 1552, smacks not so much of jealousy as an attempt to rule the roost from beyond the grave. In return for the lease of his farm William Whiting expected his wife Agnes to 'keepe herself wyddow tell Thomas my sonne be 20 yeres of Age'. Should she remarry, however, she was to give back the estate in exactly the same condition as she found it, down to the last acre of wheat, the last pewter plate, and the last chicken running about in the yard. If she did so her magnanimous husband decreed that she should have £20 'when she marryethe', along with the gift of two pairs of sheets and '*her rayment that belongeth to her backe, and go her waye*'. Furthermore, if she 'myseuse Joan [their daughter] I wyll her part be made out £10 and shee to be taken a waye from here'. And what does William Whiting do after displaying all this mistrust and suspicion? He appoints his wife to be an executor of his will!

The underlying reason behind these dictatorial attitudes (and William Whiting was by no means the only one) was not the fear that children might be ill-treated by a stepfather, although this was always a possibility. Rather, it was the desire to keep the estate together as a going concern for the son to inherit. It is noticeable that often the strictures only refer to the wife remaining a widow until the eldest son comes of age and can take over the holding in his own right. But what never seems to have entered the minds of these men is how a widow with (in Whiting's case, five) young children to bring up could possibly look after the wheat, rye and barley, the cattle, horses, poultry and the rest *without* remarrying. It was impossible, of course, and doubtless many widows ignored the wishes of their husbands, who were dead and buried in the churchyard and unable to do a thing about it.

Not all men were unreasonable, and some showed a much better appreciation of the difficulties their wives would have to face. This is William Fox, definitely 'hooll of mynde', as he said in 1522:

. . . if it forton [fortune] Johan my wif to mary herafter then I will that the man that schall marie hire shall put in sufficiant Suirtie as shalbe thought necessarie . . . for the full Redilivering of such mony and goods as I have bequeathed to John Foxe my son.

A much more commonsense approach.

The provisions made for children are as varied as the people who made them. Robert Blokke in 1549, for example, left his 'poore childerne eche of them £4 a pece and a cowe bullocke apece' as well as '4 sheep a pece of the parcell of shepe that be at Potton'. Sheep were a major source of wealth in the early sixteenth century and even the poorest villager normally had two or three to his name. You would doze off long before you had finished counting the sheep, lambs, hoggets and so forth mentioned in these wills. In an age when cash was in short supply people tended to measure their wealth in terms of the goods and chattels they owned, and they used sheep as a kind of currency.

It was usually the eldest son who inherited the bulk of an estate, normally consisting of the main dwelling house and the lion's share of the land. Where the testator was a craftsman or in some form of trade he frequently bequeathed his working tools and equipment to his eldest son, although even the most dedicated artisan was also a part-time farmer holding a few acres of land which he used to augment his slender income. Robert Myddelton received 'all my curreyng geyre' from his father in 1548, as well as 'my gryndyng stone with all thyngs perteynyng unto it'. At least some of Robert's work after his father's death was going to consist of dressing and colouring pieces of tanned leather, because that is what a currier did. Our old friend John Burley who owned the Falcon left his son:

a ledde, a mashe fatt, an yeldynge fatt, all the boltynge arks, my pott whele and pott bords.

Leads, mash vats and yielding vats were all brewing vessels; boulting arks were troughs where flour was sifted from bran. Young Thomas Burley was going to have to 'bake and brue' in order to live. The reference to the pot-wheel is a little puzzling. Did the Falcon attract rowdy customers who smashed a lot of ale jugs, or did John Burley add to his income by making and selling pots to his customers?

What did a man do if, like William Goodday, his wife was already dead and his only child a youngster unable to fend for himself? Typically the orphaned child (or children) was dumped on some handy relative whom the testator thought would look after him properly or else see him apprenticed. William Goodday, however, was not typical. His will, made in 1537, is one of the saddest I have come across. In it one can sense both his calm dignity and his no-nonsense approach to imminent death. All his goods were carefully parcelled out to friends and relatives; and how it must have hurt him to give away his wife's best apron, the only remembrance he had of her apart from the child. But his overriding concern was not with his soul, or self-pity, or regrets, but with the welfare of his beloved son Gregory.

I bequethe to Gregory Goodday my son £4 in Anngells [gold coins], which sume of £4 I will shall remayne in the hands of my brother Thomas Goodday, he to occupye the saide sume to his avauntaige so that he fynde my foresaide sonne Gregory Goodday *at schole to lerne to play at orgyns* . . .

This was a novel approach to the problem of an orphaned child. Presumably young Gregory had already shown some sort of musical ability which his proud father wanted to nurture. As this is the only instance I have found from this period of a man actually wishing to encourage his son's gifts rather than dictate the course of his life for him, it would be intriguing to know more – anything – about what happened to Gregory Goodday. Did he ever learn to 'play at orgyns'?

William Goodday also had his own aged mother to worry about. He was determined that at the very least she would have a decent burial, giving 10s. from the sale of some wood to his brother so he could 'brynge my mother to erthe when it shall please God to call for her'.

Younger sons and daughters were usually given second-best treatment, which I suppose was inevitable. Men were unwilling to break up their holdings by dividing them among their sons, so the younger boys had to make their own way in the world, assisted by as much material encouragement as their parents could afford after setting up their heir. With the poorer villagers this often meant the younger children having to make do with little more than a few sheep and as much spare cash as could be found. Even Clement Whiting, whose unpleasant but well-off father we have already met, could only expect '£10 of good and lawfull monye of Inglonde' and '2 oxen and one horse and one cow next the beste' and 'my thyrde fetherbede'. Unmarried daughters, on the other hand, were provided with what was intended to be a tempting dowry, often just a straightforward cash payment, as in the case of Thomas Hawse in 1549:

I geve also to Kateryne my daughter 40s. to be payde heyre att the daye of hayre maryage . . .

Similar arrangements were made for his other two unmarried girls. More often than not a date was included in the bequest stating exactly when the money was to be paid. In the case of boys it was generally a year or two later than for girls. George Brockewell's will is typical of many; he left £6 13s. 4d. to his daughter Audrey 'if she lyve to the aige of 18 yeres, or ells at the day of her mariage'. Many fathers obviously expected their daughters to be married before they reached eighteen.

As well as having a wife and children to think about, some men were in the awful position of having pregnant wives while they themselves were dying. Apart from the fact that they would not live to see the child, there were somewhat complicated arrangements to be made for its care. One example – a simple one – will do:

If my wyfe be with chylde I geve to the chylde 40s., and if shee be note with chylde then I gyve the 40s. to Tyme and Brygett my chyldern . . .

That was Rafe Bell from his death-bed on Monday 22 August 1552. He never did know whether his wife was pregnant or not, because within a few days of making his will he had joined the countless thousands of his village forebears in the churchyard.

I shall keep this section on houses as brief as I can because the wills become more informative later on and there is more to say then. During the first half of the sixteenth century houses were gradually becoming more comfortable – in some cases positively luxurious – when compared with their medieval predecessors. At the very bottom end of the scale nothing much had changed, and even middle-class houses were still small and retained the characteristic medieval open-hall layout. Those houses described as 'Tudor cottages' in today's estate agents' catalogues are in fact substantial yeoman farmers' houses. Few if any genuine 'cottages' survive from the Tudor period – they were much too flimsy.

In the houses of the will-making class the hall was still the most important room, often containing the table. Tables were either like the 'folte [folding] table in the halle at the cocke', as Thomas Ratford described his, or a heavy oak trestle table of the type bequeathed by Thomas Huckle when he left 'the table in the hall with the trestelle' to his wife Agnes. Also kept in the hall was the attendant furniture, such as the 'stoles, chayres, tables, potts, pannes with all other implements of howsolde' of William Goodday. Men were never very good at describing that sort of thing. Walls were sometimes decorated with painted cloths called hangings, richly coloured descendants of medieval tapestries which must have brought some welcome gaiety to the sombre rooms. Katherine Ratford evidently thought so because she had them in both parlour and hall of her house at Brook End in 1545. Some people employed itinerant artists to decorate their walls, as can still be seen in Thomas Bird's rectory today, where vestiges of early Tudor wall-paintings have recently been uncovered.

The parlour contained the other major item of furniture mentioned in the wills: the bed. Beds were treasured family possessions, passed on from generation to generation. There was often more than one. John Burley, for example, left 'a fetherbedde' each to both his daughters and another to his granddaughter, while we have already seen that Clement Whiting received his father's third-best bed. Almost as prized as the beds themselves was their accompanying 'furniture', as William Malden made plain when he left his son Thomas:

all bedsteds, tables and formes, bedhangyngs, hawlyngs and coveryngs, with my best fetherbedde with all therto belongynge exceptynge . . . one matteres, one coverlet and 2 payre of shetts . . .

William Goodday left to Isobel Brockewell, with obvious pride, 'my best fyne shette wrawght with sylke and the pyllow with the bere wrawght with sylke', which was luxury indeed.

Apart from beds and tables there was little other furniture. Clothes were kept in 'presses', an early form of wardrobe, or in sturdy chests and boxes along with other household goods. The chests and boxes also served as somewhere to sit. Surprisingly the early wills contain only four references to these everyday objects, perhaps because they *were* everyday items and thus deemed unworthy of notice. William Fox left 'a gret cofer that I did bye', William Goodday had his 'coffer with all my presse' and Katherine Ratford spoke proudly of her 'redde sprewce forcer with all that is in hit'. A forcer was a strongbox. John Nicholas tells us what was in his when he orders his executors to 'sell the 6 ells of clothe in my coffer'. He is also the only person to mention an 'almerye', a kind of cupboard.

Many utensils of one sort or another are recorded: 'my grettest brasse potte and a panne of brasse', a 'lyttell posnett with a handle', 'pewtre dysshes and platters with all maner of lattyn vessell' are all mentioned by John Nicholas. Mostly this sort of thing was dismissed by men as 'household stuff'.

Silver was not uncommon among the wealthier people, often taking the form of spoons. Joan Golde had five 'sylver spones' in her house and Richard Clark had seventeen in his, all of which were given to relatives and friends. One of Clark's bequests was of '4 sylver spones and a maser'. I think the mazer (a wooden drinking bowl) probably had a silver mount. Apart from Thomas Ancten's silver candlesticks one has to go back to Margaret Taylard's will of 1475 to find any really substantial silver ware: 'one silver bowl with cover', 'one silver salt with lid', 'a coral rosary with the paternoster [a special bead] of silver enamel' and six silver spoons. She could also afford to leave a gold ring to Elizabeth Bonyface.

Surprisingly, men seem more concerned with their clothes than women. Perhaps this is because there are more male testators, or perhaps it is because a set of clothes tended to be handed down from father to son as a kind of heirloom. A more likely reason is that the women had already decided who was to have a particular dress, hat or apron long before they ever came to make a will. Robert Barford died a bachelor in 1546 (and, incidentally, nicely illustrates my point about clothes passing from father to son) when he left 'a grene coote and a violet coote of my fathers' to William Studdall. His 'best sherte' went to John Burton, but where did the 'gowne' and the 'peticote' which he gave to his sister-in-law and sister respectively come from? Or, for that matter, the two kirtles he left? From his mother, I should think, although I do not know why he and not the women in the family got them in the first place.

What a stirring sight these men must have made in their Sunday best. I can imagine Richard Clark wearing his 'roset [russet] gowne furrede with lambe' and his 'best jacket and a wosted dublet' as he sat down in the hall at Merton Manor Farm to eat with his 'sylver spones'. I can also imagine the mess his clothes got into as he picked his way through the mud and manure in the farmyard, and the curses of his wife when she came to clean them. Some of his less-well-off contemporaries were also clothes-conscious. William Lawe with his 'chamlet Jakett' and his 'worstede Jakett', Rafe Bell fetchingly attired in 'dublett' and 'payre of hosen', John Burley in his 'blake furred gowne' and even Thomas Ancten, resplendent in his 'gowne furred with fox' and 'best doublet of worstede' were all sixteenth-century men of fashion.

Of the other types of bequests, mostly of a small and inconsequential nature, two are worthy of mention. Timber is one. It was becoming scarce by the Tudor period, and with scarcity came a rise in value. It is specifically noted in only two wills. Thomas Huckle, obviously a carpenter or wheelwright, left to his son John the 'tooles and tymbre that longeth to my occupacon', while William Goodday left his house to Thomas Fryer along with 'all my tymbre in my house to repayre the same . . . and allso a pece of tymbre lyeinge in Burtons yarde to make a kyrble for the well'.

Lastly, servants were sometimes deemed worthy of mention, but not often. Two examples: Richard Clark remembered his ex-servant Elizabeth who 'now dwellethe with Robert Bycley' with 40s. worth of affection, although what his wife had to say about it is another matter. And in a typically blunt phrase sour, dictatorial old William Whiting left a combe of barley to each of this three servants on condition they 'tarrye tyll Mychaellmas'.

When the testator had decided who should or should not benefit from his estate, he then had to consider the problem of whom he could trust to see that his wishes were carried out. There were usually two of these 'executors', often his wife and son, but sometimes close friends or the parish priest. An overseer, or supervisor, was also appointed to keep a check on the executors, and this appointment was normally filled by a trusted friend or relative. It was customary to give the overseer a small token of appreciation for undertaking what could turn out to be a difficult task, requiring

Richard Clark wearing his 'gowne furrede with lambe'

diplomacy and tact. John Basse asked William Malden to do the job and gave him 'for his labor 6s. 8d. above hys costs and expensys'. Thomas Golde in 1538 appointed Thomas Basse to be the supervisor of his will 'so yt be done and fullfylled accordynge as my will, and so to have for his labor and paynes takynge 3s. 4d.'. And however philanthropic Thomas Ancten may have been he was no fool when it came to business. His overseer was left in no doubt why he was chosen for the task. He picked:

my frende John Carleton, gentilman, to whom for his kyndenes and diligence here in to be shewed, and for the love I bere to him and Antony his sonne, I have solde all my londes and leasses for yeres in the said Towne and parishe of Gamlingay *for lesse money then I myght have had of a nother man* by £16 13s. 4d.

And under no circumstances was John Carleton getting a fee!

Now all that was left was for the scrivener to write down the names of those present as witnesses, get them to sign, or those who were illiterate to make their mark, and the will was finished. But who was the scrivener? It must frequently have been the parish priest, since few of the villagers could do anything more than scratch down their names, but with an annoying sense of modesty he usually hides behind the phrase 'with other'. And with that the testator freed himself from earthly care and was ready to meet his Maker.

11

The Bawdy Court

By the late 1550s the Reformation was virtually over. The Roman Catholic faith was no longer the state religion. The establishment of the Church of England changed the thinking of ordinary men and women all over the country – not overnight, but over perhaps ten, twenty or thirty years. At first it must have seemed very confusing. They were ordered to remove 'superstitious images', brasses and so on, from their churches, then, under Mary, they were told to put them all back, only to find that with the accession of Elizabeth to the throne in 1558 they must all be removed again. Religious zeal in the form of Puritanism was given its head, becoming the driving force behind much of English life during the following century. Much that was rotten and corrupt was swept away and also, in the nature of such things, much that was not. The guilds (and their charitable deeds) disappeared for ever, their possessions sold off to men hungry for land. No more masses were sung in Gamlingay church, villagers no longer left money in their wills to the bells or for the saying of obits, and there were no more icons and other symbols of religious belief which had sustained the medieval church. Some of the magic, both literally and metaphorically, had gone from common people's lives.

How much this chopping and changing affected the people of Gamlingay I have no way of knowing. Probably they adapted to the new ways quickly enough; perhaps they were just indifferent. Certainly there is no trace of any reaction in the records. But there was one way in which the village was changed by the Reformation, and that was in the matter of land.

Following the confiscations of Church property came the biggest boom in the land market the country had ever seen. Millions of acres acquired new owners as the king sold off the spoils of his pillaging. In Gamlingay the Sawtry Abbey estate, the land of St Neots Monastery, the guildhall and small parcels of land belonging to the guild of the Trinity, as well as sundry plots belonging to other religious foundations were put up for sale. Some of it ended up in the hands of up-and-coming yeoman families in the village – the Apthorpes and the Russells, for instance, whom we shall meet soon – and no doubt it helped them in their remorseless climb up the social ladder. I think that they probably would have clawed their way up soon enough even without the release of so much land onto the market; the sales simply speeded the process up a bit.

When people decide to change any institution that they feel has outlived its usefulness there is often a tendency to push too far in the opposite direction. So it was with the Church. I have a lot of sympathy with the Puritans, those much-maligned characters of history, but I have to admit that sometimes in their concern for the moral welfare of their flock their actions seemed more ridiculous than sublime. As a result of the puritanical streak which now ran down the backbone of the Church of England, churchwardens were actively encouraged to spy on their neighbours. All kinds of village tittle-tattle, half-truth and rumour was repeated with official approval and elevated to the status of 'evidence'. It is not surprising that before very long the Church courts were full to overflowing with the victims of scandalised rumour-mongers.

'Church courts' is perhaps an odd phrase to modern ears and requires some explanation. The Church exercised jurisdiction over the probate (proving) of wills, over marriage and divorce, offences against Church laws and spiritual matters generally, including the tricky area of morality. In Cambridgeshire this jurisdiction was divided between the archdeacon and the bishop of Ely, with Gamlingay (as a part of

Bourn deanery) covered by the archdeacon. Presentments of offences both real and imagined were made to the archdeacon during his parochial visitations. If possible, they were based on fact, but presentments could be made on 'common fame' (rumour) and 'vehement suspicion'. Cases arising from them were heard in Cambridge. The court usually imposed some form of penance or a fine or simply a warning on those found guilty. Excommunication was reserved for those who failed to turn up at the hearing or who were found guilty of grave offences. Since much of the court's time was taken up with cases of sexual aberration it is easy to see why the Church courts were known throughout the land as the 'Bawdy Courts'. The following presentments are taken from the Ely diocesan records kept in the University Library in Cambridge. They cover a period of fifty years:

Margaret Warren: 'for absentinge hir sellf from hir husband, he being very syck'.

James Meade: 'for scoldinge'.

Thomas Basse: 'kepeth the Comunion Cup in his hands and that he hath not delivered his Accompts of the Churchwardenshippe for the last yere'.

John Wrighte: 'begatte his woman sarvante with childe'.

Katherine Radcliffe: 'hathe ben in our towne above the space of A monethe and have not come to the Churche'.

John Wilson: 'for lyving suspiciouslye with An Remson, beinge unmaried'.

Alice Bestowe, widow: 'for six bushells of corne that dothe belonge to the towne; she will nether pay the corne nor the rent for it'.

John Bretherton: 'vehemently suspected to have comitted fornication before mariage'.

John Robinson: 'for useinge himselfe disorderly in the time of comon prayres, in that *he did laughe and kicke with his legges*'.

The churchwardens: 'for that the Towne commandments be decayed'.

John Goodin and Lucy Robinson: 'for beinge marryed uppon Tewsday in Whitsun weeke last, marryeinge tyme then beinge oute'.

John Cockerell: 'hath not recived the Communion with us this Easter'.

Thomas Cater, curate: 'whether he be licensed or noe we cannott tell'.

Christopher Mead: 'for incontinencie before mariage'.

The village gossips had never had such an opportunity to tell tales about their fellow villagers under a cloak of authorised respectability. The tut-tutting must have been all the louder when someone like Thomas Condall was hauled before the court and charged that 'the common fame ys that he shoulde be noughte with Agnes Ludloe, alias Trewelove, his Auntes daughter'. The inference is that he had slept with Agnes, a charge he stoutly denied, saying that he had been out of the area on his master's business and was about to go again, thinking it would be 'aboute Sturbrydge Fayre or Michelmas next before he come home againe'. Rather an obtuse, not to say feeble, excuse, but the court seems to have swallowed it. Bonyface Wragge was charged the same year (1576) with refusing to pay the fine for not attending church, and for having 'kepte men in his howse in tyme of service'. His answer both admits the charge and misses the point with almost the same dexterity as Thomas Condall, stating 'they were his verye frends and strangers that came to make merrye there with him'.

Where some form of penance was ordered by the court this usually involved the guilty person being exposed to public ridicule in such a way as to make him or her so chastened by the experience that they would never repeat the offence. It did not work particularly well in practice, human nature being what it is, but it must have been a mollifying experience all the same. Margaret Person, a 'disquieter' of holy service, was ordered to kneel in the middle alley of the church during the service and in a loud voice speak these words:

Good people, I do acknowledge and confesse that I have mysused and muche unreverently behaved my self in this holy place at the tyme of devyne service, to the great offence of allmighty God and evell example of you all.

That was humiliating enough, but the penalty for fornication was much tougher. Thomas Kendricke, in 1570, was told to stand

3 severall Sundays or holydays in a white shete and a wand in his hand, in the church porch there from the second peale to morninge prayre untill the readinge of the second lesson, and then the vicar to fetche him in with the Psalme of Miserere in Englishe.

Solemn moralising on the sexual mores of other people has long been a failing of the righteous. There is no sound more grating, even four centuries later, than that of people casting stones. And is it a coincidence that very few members of the gentry or the upper classes were ever carted off to the ecclesiastical courts? No, they were too powerful or well-connected for the archdeacon to cross. Either that or they led blameless lives.

Tucked away among the pile of diocesan records in the University Library is a small, slim volume consisting entirely of lists of people excommunicated in Cambridgeshire between the years 1571 and 1584. The scribe has written in it the following matter-of-fact details of a triple excommunication from 1582 which is surely the strangest case of all:

Thomas Upchurche: 'hathe married another mans wief'.

Edward Scayles: 'for selling of his sayd wief (viz. Issabell Bowers) to Thomas Upchurche for 16s.'.

Issabell Bowers for the same reason.

Perhaps I may suggest you reread those few lines again if, like me when I first saw it, you cannot believe your eyes. Why did they do it? I could hazard a guess or two but they are likely to be as far from the truth as we are in time from the participants. I have not come across another case like it, although I do know of two betrothed Essex women who were sold during this period. Their combined valuation did not match that of Isabell Bowers, and even she was only considered to be worth about the same as a second-rate horse. Wife-sales were held, it is true, in the eighteenth and nineteenth centuries but I think that in this case there is a parallel with those Essex women, albeit one that does not bring us any closer to answering the question 'why?'. The clue lies in the word 'betrothed'.

Marriage in a legal sense was, until the 1754 Marriage Act, composed of five separate stages. The first was the contract arranged between the respective parents concerning the dowry and other financial matters. When that was completed to everyone's satisfaction the couple exchanged verbal promises (they 'plighted their troth' and were therefore 'betrothed') and it was this stage that constituted legal marriage. Then followed the proclamation of the banns in church, after which the Church gave its formal blessing to the union at the wedding ceremony within the parish church. In the sixteenth century the church was attempting to have this fourth stage recognised as the lawful moment of marriage. The final stage, which was probably superfluous according to the village gossip recorded by the courts, was the consummation. Put simply, the exchange of phrases more or less similar to 'I take thee for my wife/husband', if performed before witnesses, was recognised as constituting marriage.

This was the ceremony Edward Scayles and Isabell Bowers had performed. The only difference between them and the Essex women was in terminology. They had all been through the same ceremony and were legally married. This also explains why Isabell Bowers kept her maiden name (at least, I *think* it does) and also why the Church excommunicated her and Edward Scayles as a married couple. Not perfect, I must admit, but it is the best explanation I have.

At the risk of 'casting stones' myself, there is a later case, from the court records of 1601, which throws a little more light on the lady in question. She was presented 'for havinge a childe by Richard Brite, as she sayeth'. What that does or does not prove is a matter I leave to the reader. The whole affair is a mystery. All I can add is that Thomas Upchurche and Isabell Bowers remained in the village, but Edward Scayles did not.

12

John Russell

During the years I have been gathering the raw material for this book I have come across a number of historical characters I would like to have met. There are also some I would not like to have bumped into on a dark night, and a few I would have avoided during daylight. There are those like the Fishers of the early fifteenth century whom it must have been unpleasant to antagonise. Then there are the Anctens, who I feel could be trusted instinctively, and William Purchase, another 'old friend'.

Then there is John Russell. John Russell was astute, kind-hearted, and had that roguish Elizabethan rough-and-tumble attitude to life which characterised some of his more illustrious contemporaries. His family was one of the foremost in the village from the middle of the fifteenth until the early seventeenth century, building up considerable wealth and gaining some powerful enemies. Remember Thomas Russell, beaten up by Edward Langton, several of his servants and a 'bandog' in 1492. John Russell modestly described himself as a husbandman in his will, but the evidence it contains points to a higher social position. He owned a mill, an inn, three houses, and land and sheep in Gamlingay and Waresley. He also possessed a fatal attraction for women – or perhaps it was the other way round. Russell had married Joan Parson, a widow, by 1559 at the latest, because according to the Patent Rolls of that year she was pardoned for certain unspecified crimes at a cost to her purse of 26s. 8d. Dozens of other people were pardoned for the same thing at the same time, which probably merely means she was a Catholic. As well as the material benefits she may have brought with her Mrs Russell presented her new husband with a ready-made family – five girls and three boys from her first marriage.

I like John Russell for precisely the reasons that his wife, in all honesty, probably did not. What her feelings were when her husband was first named in the ecclesiastical court is anyone's guess. Katherine Nelson was presented on the 25 May 1569 because she 'did sclander John Russell and Agnes Ward togither'. Having seen the kind of village gossip regularly reported to the court one can easily imagine what the slander was. Agnes Ward swore her innocence and was let off. But 'no smoke without fire', as they say, and a month later Russell himself was presented. This time the reason is made crystal clear:

he was taken in bedd with Elizabethe Anderson, and there so taken by Martyn Kevell, William Kevell and Robert Pygot.

One can easily picture the scene: the horrified trio come upon the unsuspecting lovers *in flagrante*, and feeling duty bound to report the matter rush off in mortification to tell all to the outraged churchwardens. But one would be wrong because a mere two days later Martin Kevell was presented because he had 'committed fornicacion with Elizabethe Anderson'. A different picture begins to emerge. It now sounds as if Kevell and Anderson were lovers, and that Elizabeth Anderson was deceiving him. Kevell discovered her in bed with John Russell and in a fit of jealous rage reported the pair of them to the authorities. Russell got his revenge by reporting Kevell. Joan Russell probably exacted her own form of revenge on her erring husband when she discovered what had been going on. I admit this is only one of several possible scenarios, but it seems the most likely to me.

I hope I am not being unfair when I say that I think Elizabeth Anderson was one of the village prostitutes. Certainly the next woman linked with John Russell in the church courts was. In 1570 he was presented 'uppon a sclander therove the Towne, of hordam with Sybbyll Carton', which was put more plainly when the presentation was repeated later on: 'that he comytted whoredome with Sybill

Carton'. Russell was ordered to purge himself 'twelve-handed': that is, to find five people plus himself to swear his innocence. Sybil Carton was found guilty and suffered the usual form of penance in the church porch 'in a white shete, barefaced, with a white wand in hir hand three severall Sundays', and so forth.

After this case Russell seems to have become a reformed character as he was not presented again – although it could just be that he was more careful with his extramarital relationships. Or perhaps his wife's reaction to his bed-hopping put him off. Martin Kevell appears once more, in 1570, for 'suspiciously being with Elizabeth Andrewe', a statement which can only mean one thing.

Russell died in 1588, the year of the Armada. His will, now in the Public Record Office, offers some further clues to his personality. Judging from the first bequest he could be both kind and generous:

I doe give to William Randall, alias Russell, *whiche I have brought upp of a childe*, three roodes of Land att millbridge in Gamlingaye whiche the windmill doethe stand uppon and the windmill withe all manner of implements therunto belonginge. . .

Was William Randall, alias Russell, the result of an earlier liaison with one of the accommodating village women? If he was, and given the awkwardness of the situation, then the Russells both deserve credit for raising the child, Joan especially.

As well as women, Russell also enjoyed more than the occasional sup of ale. The following bequest is typical of the man and shows he was quite capable of combining a solemn Church ritual with an irreverent booze-up. To Thomas and John Bestow he left

my house at milbridge and the grounde inclosed wherin the howse doethe stand, payinge yearly thre shillings fower pence *to be bestowed on a drinkinge at Gangtide* under the banck in Potton waye, nere unto the house.

John Russell's thoughtful 'drinkinge', given to the parishioners as they perambulated the village bounds on the annual 'Gangtide' or Rogation processions, enlivened an already colourful scene and quenched the thirst of villagers grown hot and dusty with a good deal of walking. I should imagine the name of John Russell was well toasted each year.

The Cock today

He left no children of his own – legitimate ones, anyway – and the gift of a house to his step-grandson and the numerous small bequests to his step-children and step-grandchildren seem further evidence of his generous nature.

I suppose every lover of good ale must dream of owning his own pub. John Russell achieved that dream (and perhaps it also gave him somewhere to conduct his not-so-private affairs). To his nephew Thomas Russell he left 'my house called the cock' with some land on the understanding that 20s would be spent on the poor in Gamlingay at Christmas and Easter each year. There was a similar provision for the poor of neighbouring Waresley. Once again the same generosity, once again an attempt to jolly along Church ritual. Thomas Russell was also asked to provide for a 'memoriall to be paynted and sett upp on the howse ende of the Cock to continue in Gamlingaye for ever', but unless my eyes deceive me Thomas conveniently overlooked this when his uncle was dead. Either that, or the sign which still exists, moulded into the exterior plasterwork of the Cock and coyly described by the Royal Commission on Historical Monuments as 'convivial emblems' is that memorial. And a rather appropriate one it would be.

To conclude this brief portrait I would like to quote a list which appears at the end of Russell's will. It shows that as well as a generous nature he had that nose for business that every successful Elizabethan needed to have. Even when he lay dying John Russell knew exactly what was owed to him, by whom and for what:

Debtes owinge unto me, John Russell:
Humfrey Fox owethe me 14s. for a quarter of barlye and 5s. for plowinge and 19s.
Walter Moodey owethe me for a calfe 6s.
Thomas Basse of Gamlingay owethe me 26s 8d.
Richard Stocker owethe me 20s.
Hughe Lamderde owethe me 10s.
Andrewe Mitten owethe me £10.
William Lyllis owethe me £3 10s. 0d.
Thomas Condall owethe me for a horse 53s. 4d.
Lawrence Carter owethe me £10 13s. 4d.
Walter Parson owethe me 20s.
Thomas Malden the elder owethe me 40s. And for a quarter of barley 13s.
Nicholas Fanne owethe me 24s.
Michaell Lymer owethe me 3s. 4d.
For carryinge of wood that was betwixt Robert Waters and his parte 18d.

Nearly all those seem to have been straight cash loans. I like to think of John Russell ending his days by lending some of his spare cash to his needy neighbours. In fact, as I said, I just like John Russell.

13

Wills Again

Now I have returned to the subject of wills I may as well stay with them and examine the forty-two which survive from the years 1554 to 1600. They show many changes from the earlier ones.

For a start there are no longer references to the Blessed Virgin Mary and fewer to 'all the hollie companie of hevyn'. Instead, the testator is usually full of confidence in his salvation 'through my saviour and Redemer Jesus Christ', reflecting the changeover from Catholicism to Protestantism. More striking than this is the increase in personal wealth of the will-making section of the village, and with it the tendency to use cash for small bequests instead of the sheep and suchlike so frequently used before. Without quoting the total value and composition of each testator's estate it is rather difficult to show this difference. Mary Ratford (1576) was typical of this transitional period when she left her two brothers 'twoo shepe and twentie shillings in money' and her mother-in-law 'fyve shepe, one Calf and tenne shillings'. Slightly less typical is the 'pursse and 2 ryalles of goulde in it' belonging to John Hobbs seven years earlier. A ryal was a gold coin worth (at this time) 15s.

William Farye, 'yeoman, Crased in bodye but of a verye goode and perfecte memorye' gave the vicar, John Claveringe, in 1595, 'three Gynniers of goulde inclosed in one, in remembrance of my good will towards him'. It is a puzzling bequest, because it was to be another seventy years before the first guinea was minted. Perhaps it was 'guilders' that Farye had in mind. I do not suppose that John Claveringe minded what they were – gold was gold, no matter what shape or form it came in.

John Massye was a well-off outsider who had moved to the village from the London area. In his will dated 1593 he left his sisters Anne and Sara 40 marks and £20 respectively, while to his 'good maister Mr Richard Tramton' he gave 'two Angels of goulde to make a goulde ringe, and to my Mistress his wyef likewise two Angels of gould'. Richard Nicholas ('my lovinge frend and landlorde') received the same. The giving of rings at a funeral as a remembrance of the deceased was quite common among the wealthier classes. The poor went to their humble graves with no such trappings.

Almost every will mentions the poor. This was partly a reaction to their increasing numbers – a problem that eventually became acute – and partly also that charitable spirit which had previously found expression in the gifts of money, goods and land to the church and the parish guilds. The practice was also recommended by the state. For instance, Robert Clark, a baker, gave 'unto the poore of Gamlingaye a Coombe of wheate to be baked and distrybuted amongst them imediatly after my decease'. That was in 1600. A year earlier Gilbert Cowper had been more specific. The £20 he left was for:

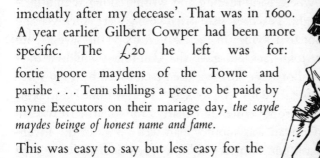

fortie poore maydens of the Towne and parishe . . . Tenn shillings a peece to be paide by myne Executors on their mariage day, *the sayde maydes beinge of honest name and fame.*

This was easy to say but less easy for the executors to carry out.

I wish I knew who first suggested the idea of providing an alms-house for the village poor. It is first mentioned in 1559 when William Harmer left 8d.

to the 'Reparasions of the almose howse', giving the impression that it was already well-established. But when, ten years later, John Hobbs said 'I geve to the making of the almosse house in Gamlingay 20s., *if the said almysse house be set up*', was there an almshouse or not? Hobbs's widow gave 6s. 8d. to repair the 'alums howse' two years later, which further confuses the matter. Richard Jacob ('gent') was no clearer about it in his will dated 1577. It contains a bequest of 40s. 'towardes the buildinge *or* reparacons of the Almes howse'. In contrast, John Massye's bequest of 1593 is quite clear.

I bequeathe twentie nobles to be bestowed to the best and most profitable use of the power people of Gamlingay, either by buildinge of one Almes howse or otherwise as shall seme good . . .

Things rumbled on like that until 1665, when the problem was solved once and for all by the building of the present almshouses by John Jacob. The fact that so many people considered one necessary at least a hundred years earlier indicates how much of a headache the poor were becoming.

The village school is another rather ethereal village institution. Dozens of the larger Cambridgeshire villages possessed a school of some description where basic reading and writing along with a little grammar were taught. Teachers were often young clergymen waiting for an appointment to a living. In the early years of the seventeenth century the vicar, John Jackson, gave the Gamlingay children their lessons. But a school of some sort had been established by 1559 when William Harmer instructed his wife to 'kepe my sone Edmond to skole for one yere at hare proper costes and charges for to larne to wryght and Rede'. John Condall was another man well aware of the advantages that even a basic education could bring a boy, and willed in 1563 that 'my 2 sones to be kept at skoole untill the age of 18, and that they shall lack nether meat nor drink nor anything . . .'.

John Hedding declared his interest in education by saying 'I give to be distributed emong schollers of Gamlyngaye 12d.'. He was one of those rare people who always consider others to be less fortunate than themselves, and he spent a good deal of time in his will helping them. These are some examples of his kindness. Note the tiny amounts of cash involved:

I give to the repayringe of the church 12d.
I give to Father Clorse my one old cote.
I give to Dixon 1d. and a Jerkyn.
I give to Stodole an old paire of hose.
I give to Thomas Tyler, Humfrie Esemante and to William Tyler, to either of them 1d.
I give to Thomas Huckle, vicare, 12d.

His wife was to receive the lease of his house, his eldest sone Thomas was given half an acre of barley 'readie sowen', and 'my busshell, my grynston so that he paye the 12d. to the churche', as well as his 'sieth' and 3d. as executor. His other son John received his father's 'best cote, a Jerkyn, a flexen shirte'. So old John Hedding, who had but a humble house, 5s. in cash, a few old clothes, some tools, three or four sheep and two tiny plots of land managed to put to shame some of the better-off villagers by his simple good-natured charity.

When I read these bequests and think of all the work it must have meant for the executors, I am tempted to wonder whether they were all carried out as requested. But this is being cynical: two men noted specifically that they were literally doing the will of others. John Hitt, in 1575; 'Marye my wyeff shall paye unto my 2 sonnes John Hytt and Richard Hytt 9 quarters of barlye betwene them, and to either of them 20s., *which was gyven unto them by the last will of their unkell Clement Whitinge*'. Thomase Basse was made supervisor of Richard Berry's will in 1526. Thirty years later, Basse instructed in his own will that an obit be kept yearly for Berry *'as the wyll of Beriy do speake'*. Basse was not to know that two years later when Elizabeth was crowned there would be no more obits.

The wife of a later Thomas Basse – Helen – neatly summed up the contemporary attitude of men towards women in 1573. She disarmingly admitted that her last will and testament was made 'with the licence and consent of my husbande Thomas Baysse, which hath sett his hand unto the same . . .'. She does not seem to have been particularly upset by having to ask permission to write her own will (it was in fact a legal requirement). Perhaps her husband was more understanding than most. Her will, incidentally, contains the fullest reference to the things a woman brought with her as part of her 'portion' when she married. To her daughter Elizabeth she gave 'my stuffe that I bowghte, that is to saye, twoo paire sheitts, a kirtle, the best frocke, my best petticott, a fyne kercher, a neckercher'.

Just as revealing of the attitude of men is this, from Robert Clark. Directing his wife, he says:

sheç shall at the tyme of her death *geve all her goods to her frends and myne together* at her discretion [!], equally to be devided emongst them.

I call that taking husbandly command to the limit.

A husband was of course still very much concerned with his wife's future. We have seen before how William Whiting laid down harsh and exacting conditions if his wife remarried. The will of his son Thomas illustrates very well the slowly changing attitudes. He left his wife an annuity of £3 6s. 8d. and her board with their son-in-law, as well as half his linen (their linen?) and a featherbed. If she should happen to 'mislike of her abideinge and boord' the son-in-law was to pay her £6 13s. 4d. a year, and she was to have 'duringe her liffe the Chamber over the buttrie in my nowe dwellinge howse' along with two acres of land and pasture for a cow. But the biggest change of all is this: should she remarry the bequest becomes void (except for the bed and linen) and instead she is to have the enormous sum of £40 as a gift – a case of the sins of the father not going unnoticed.

Thomas Whiting's will raises another matter which it is as well to mention here. Whiting's nephew Robert Griggs was given a strip of land on which the executors were told to

erecte and builde a house upon the same grownde, with a Chymney and twoo roomes . . . wherof Robert Griggs . . . shall yerelie give to the poore people of the Towne of Gamlingay at the perambulation one busshell of malt to be brewed in drinke and one dozen of breade . . . at a place commonly called Stubbe Crosse.

That was written in 1596, right in the middle of the period known as the 'great rebuilding'. Were I writing about virtually any other village in southern England the story of that rebuilding would be relatively straightforward. One significant event prevents it being so in the case of Gamlingay. This event (I do not want to spoil the story) will have to wait until a later chapter, but it does mean that the story of the rebuilding will have to be split into two parts.

You will have gathered by now that for a large proportion of the population, but by no means all of it, living standards improved steadily throughout the Tudor period, particularly from 1540 onwards. There were many reasons for this: stable government and relative peace helped, but probably the biggest single factor was the change in the basic economic facts of life concerning freeholders, of which Gamlingay had many. Due to inflation, these yeomen of England were in the envious position of having continually rising selling prices for their produce; at the same time they enjoyed security of tenure and low rents, many of which had been fixed way back in the Middle Ages. Given such an encouraging state of affairs it was not beyond the wit of even the dimmest, most unbusinesslike man to collect a healthy stock of money. He then spent it, of course, because that is what money is for. Cautiously at first, buying up a few pieces of land here and there, adding a sheep or two to the flock, and so on. Then, as his confidence grew, he started to lavish his money on a more luxurious lifestyle. From around 1570 until about 1640 the whole of eastern and southern England was transformed by this new prosperity. Standards of housing which were perfectly adequate only a generation before became as out of date in a Tudor village as an overcrowded Victorian slum would be in ours. People wanted more comfortable houses to live in and thousands of houses were altered and improved, or knocked down and better ones built in their place.

The usual way of modernising an old medieval open-hall house was to put a ceiling over the hall and insert a chimney, thus virtually doubling the available living area. In Gamlingay, for example, this was done in the two houses built by Thomas Bird a hundred years earlier. Both the rectory and Merton Manor Farm have inserted ceilings, but they also gained extra space by having a new wing built on, transforming them from L-shaped plans into H-shaped ones.

Rebuilding from the ground up gave people the chance to build in a grander style. Thomas Whiting's will, which I have just quoted, shows that even a tiny two-roomed cot had a chimney. Chimneys and upstairs rooms were now the norm. Complete rebuilding was often necessary, given the lack of repair complained about in the fifteenth-century manorial records. Many medieval houses were at the end of their useful lives anyway. Whitehall, the Burley's 'Falcon', was one

The Emplins today

such. It was in such disrepair in 1585 that Merton College leased it without demanding the usual entry-fine on condition that the new tenant made 'good and sufficient re-edifying and building of the same'.

Even such humble items as pots and pans reflect the new prosperity. Alice Mason, a widow who died in 1584, left her son Thomas 'one masure edged with silver and a pewter bason', while her other son got the rest of the pewter 'excepting fowre pewter platters'. And I can easily imagine William Roger (1554) taking a long swig from his 'pewter pinte pott' after a day spent hammering and sweating in his blacksmith's shop. Some people eschewed pewter, like William Welles (1555), who describes his 'brasse panne with brode brynks and a kettill with a baile', and Abraham Jacob, who received 'twoo Saultes and a standinge Cupp of silver and guilte' from his father Richard.

Chests and coffers are as much in evidence as before, so one reads of 'my little cofer with all the Lynnen therein', for instance, and 'one hutche under the wyndowe' – the usual place to keep them, where they could double as seats – and 'my great read cheste'. I am intrigued by Gilbert Cowper's reference to 'my Coffer and all in it unbequeathed, *my wrightings onlie excepted*', which he left to John Bestow in 1599. Was he a budding author, perhaps, or a diarist? It is idle to speculate, but since he left the 'wrightings' to his executors I should think they were deeds or legal documents of some kind.

Sleeping arrangements had changed little since the Middle Ages. Despite their blankets, bolsters, pillows, coverlets, mattresses and occasional fine silk, most people still slept downstairs as their fathers and grandfathers had done before them. It took some time before the new chambers upstairs were used for anything other than storage. Children or servants often slept in the same room as the master of the house on a small bed on wheels which could be rolled under the main bed when not in use. Gilbert Cowper described the one he owned as a 'trusle bedd' but they were more commonly known as truckle, or trundle, beds.

The 'furniture' belonging to the beds is still lovingly described by many testators, but I will content myself with quoting just one example. It comes from the will of Nicholas Ratford, written in 1586. He left his daughter Audrey 'a fetherbedd, a bedstedd, twoo pillowes, a boulster, a blankett, a coverlett and six paire of sheetts, twoo of them flaxen, two taw hempen and twoo harden'. Anyone who knows how coarse those materials are will realise how uncomfortable Elizabethan sheets could be.

Thomas Basse the elder was an exception to the general rule about sleeping downstairs. Although he was in his mid-seventies he was abreast of the times, because he left his wife Joan 'all the hangyngs of the over chamber with bedsted' in 1556. Whether old Thomas managed to clamber upstairs to sleep every night is a question without answer. Incidentally, his will contains an interesting little aside. Concerning the bed he left his granddaughter Anne he decreed that his wife, and son should have the use of it *'if any of their frends do cum to them'* until Anne was old enough to marry. This informative will also includes an excellent description of the furniture to be found in more comfortable village houses. Thomas Basse had 'a cuppord in the haull, a foulte table with forme, a benche-bord, a chayer in the chamber in betwyne the dores, a prese [press], a cover and all the hangyngs in the same chamber, a bedsted, a payer of cobyerons [cob irons] and the begest spitt'. Chairs were just beginning to replace benches. Furniture was usually well-made, often of oak, and very solid.

And finally on this subject, a reference unique in these wills. It comes from Robert Gyllson in 1557, who left Steven Russell *'my chayer of eysment'*, thus providing the only evidence I have about this very important item of furniture. Every household must have had one, or something similar. Many folk no doubt made do with an everyday chamberpot. Gyllson's chair of easement was a more impressive object – an early example of a commode, in fact – which is why it is singled out for special mention. I would love to know how Steven Russell accepted his unusual gift, the only one he got from Gyllson. Was he pleased to receive it, or did he take it as some sort of veiled insult?

There are, of course, dozens of references to clothes. The majority still occur in men's wills as before, but there is now more evidence of female fashion due to the increasing number of wills made by women. It would be tiresome to quote them all, but this is how one woman, Alice Mason in 1584, disposed of her clothes:

unto Elizabeth my mayde . . . one neckerchiff with one Apron.
unto Johane Carrington my olde frocke, and an other which I weare I gyve unto Johane Malyn.
unto Alyce Marham one kerchiff with one neckerchiff.
I give to goodwyef Waters my best hatt.
And my hatt which I weare I give to goodwyef Burdall.
I geve to goodwyef Burley a kerchiff and a neckerchiff, and to everie one of her daughters a neckerchiff.

Clothes are frequently described in terms which give a good idea of their condition. Helen Basse had her 'fyne kercher', 'newe Appron', 'olde redd petycote' and a 'playne neckercher', for example, while William Welles left 'a gowne that was Custars', 'my best coote', 'my grene cote' and 'my murrey cote'.

As was the case with John Russell, many testators tacked a list of debts they were owed onto the end of their will. It was not unusual for a debtor to be 'forgiven' the money as an act of kindness or friendship, or because the testator felt it was unlikely the money would ever be recovered. Conversely, lots of people bequeathed goods to their creditors in payment for money owed. Rafe Sherwood (1589) left his son, 'my wosted Jackett and a chamlett Jackett, and one buffe Jerkyn' on condition that he paid William Stonnes of St Neots the money owed him, 'the which is aboute 30s., or betwene thyrtie shillings and fowre nobles'. This probably left the son out of pocket. Rafe Sherwood was in fact rather mean. Requesting Thomas Hedding to be the supervisor of his will he gave him 'twoo shillings, the which

Gilbert Coper oweth me', leaving Hedding the difficult task of recovering the money. This is not the only odd payment given to an overseer or supervisor: William Huckle's overseer received 'for his paynes, a swarme of bees'!

14

Manorial Descents

It is time to take a quick look at what was happening to the four major landholdings in the village. We left them in 1501, when Merton College owned Merton manor, Thomas St George owned Avenel's manor, Woodbury belonged to Audrey Delves, and the Cistercians of Sawtry Abbey still had their hands on the Shackledon estate.

Changes were afoot, however. Sawtry Abbey's grip on Shackledon was shaken off at the dissolution of the monasteries in the 1530s and was replaced by the tighter grasp of Henry VIII. Like most of the Church property he seized it was quickly sold, the purchaser being Richard Williams, alias Cromwell, whose family would prove troublesome to certain of Henry's descendants. He in turn sold it for a quick profit in 1538 to John Burgoyne and his son Thomas. The Burgoyne family still owned it at the end of the sixteenth century, when it belonged to Thomas's son, another John.

Meanwhile, Woodbury had passed to Audrey Delve's daughter Ellen. She was married to a colourful if ultimately unfortunate knight called Sir Robert Sheffield. He had fought with Henry VII against Lambert Simnel, the pretender to the throne, at the Battle of Stoke in 1487 and was knighted for his trouble. He became an MP, and eventually Speaker of the House of Commons in 1512.

His downfall came in 1515. During the Richard Hunne affair (a minor scandal of the time) Sheffield was instrumental in persuading the young King Henry VIII that his royal prerogative was threatened by the clergy. The King followed Sheffield's advice and won a small victory at the clergy's expense. It was probably a part of the softening-up process that led eventually to the break with Rome. Sheffield became a marked man in the eyes of the Church and Cardinal Wolsey soon found a way of having him clapped in the Tower of London. Henry could quite easily have had him released but chose not to, and poor Sheffield died still locked up.

In all honesty, I do not think that many Gamlingay fold gave two hoots what happened to him: Sheffield was not a popular man. He had been in charge of Woodbury for a long time, in fact if not in title, and was responsible for its enclosure in 1492/3, when he threw out a dozen families, caused two ploughs to become redundant and made over the arable land to grass. As usual the reason was money. Grazing a flock of sheep brought in more money than arable land.

After Sheffield's death the estate was inherited by his son, another Sir Robert, who died in 1531. Yet another unseemingly scramble followed before the property eventually went to his son Edmond Sheffield, later created Lord Sheffield. Lord Sheffield's son inherited it in 1549, and the estate was eventually sold by his grandson to John Manchell of Hackney in 1591.

We left Avenel's at the turn of the sixteenth century with Thomas St George, so conveniently 'acraysed of a Surfett' on the day of Edward Slade's arrest in 1532. The surfeit did him no lasting harm because he soldiered on until 1540, when he died at the advanced age of sixty-eight. His second son Francis sold Avenel's and some land in Hatley to Henry Brograve, who in turn sold it to John Gill. Gill could obviously see the manor for what it had become: a run-down, dilapidated farm (a process started by the Avenels) and it was no doubt with some relief that he sold it in 1599. The buyer was none other than Merton College, who paid £1,830 to obtain about another third of the parish. Added to their existing manor, this meant that the College now owned a large proportion of village land and all of Gamlingay wood. The fact that Avenel's manorial buildings were falling to pieces was irrelevant, because Merton could administer both estates through their existing manor and its long-established manorial machinery.

From our point of view this is wonderful news. At long last the enormous gaps in the documentation of Avenel's come to an end. Not immediately, however. One learns little about the nuts and bolts of manorial affairs in the sixteenth century from Merton's records since the documents which would have proved most useful – the court Rolls – have not survived. It is a serious problem, not remedied until the rolls begin again early in the next century.

15

The Lamentable Accident

Fire!

Along with plague and famine, fire was a recurring nightmare for most English people throughout most of their history. Wooden houses roofed with thatch, surrounded by wooden barns and outbuildings roofed with thatch, were tinder-boxes waiting for a spark. The primitive fire-service would at best give scant protection against the flames, and if a fire really took hold there was little anyone could do. Many, if not all, towns and villages have suffered at least one major fire. That of London in 1666 is the best known. Gamlingay's occurred sixty-six years earlier.

The only account of this disaster that I have been able to trace is included in the published Acts of the Privy Council for 1600. Sitting on the morning of Sunday 25 May at the court in Greenwich, the Privy Council included in its number the Chancellor of the Exchequer, the Lord Chief Justice and 'Mr Secretary Cecile', otherwise Robert Cecil, in effect Queen Elizabeth's Prime Minister. This inner circle of advisers handled most of the day-to-day affairs of state. Among other business at this sitting they directed that a letter be sent to Sir Thomas Egerton, Lord Keeper of the Great Seal of England. This is the important part of that letter (stresses and punctuation are mine):

Whereas divers of the Justices of the Peace in the countie of Cambridge have certyfied us the lamentable accydent that hath fallen upon the inhabitantes of Gamlingay in the said countie, by casualltie of fire that happned on the 21st daie of Aprill last, *whereby the moste parte of the said towne to the nomber of 76 houses with divers barnes and stackes of corne were suddainlie consumed.* By which meanes the poore inhabitantes there are brought to greate extremytie and are unable of themselves to re-edyfie those howses that were thus consumed, or to releeve themselves, theire wyves and children. And therefore they have made humble suite unto her Majestie that some charitable course might be taken for a contribucion to be made in the counties adjoynynge, towardes the buildinge up of those howses that were so consumed by the violence of the fire, and for theire releefe in their lamentable dystresse.

I am afraid I do not believe that figure of seventy-six houses destroyed, and neither, I suspect, did the Privy Council. There were barely more houses 300 years later when the population had greatly increased; perhaps the total included those 'divers barnes' as well. A little pardonable exaggeration was used to sway the Privy Council into giving the village some practical help in its hour of need.

The Council granted the request for a 'contribucion' from neighbouring counties, but I have found just one instance of any money actually being collected, although there were probably many similar tiny sums forwarded to the village in the months that followed. A paragraph in *East Anglian Notes and Queries* (1897/8) records the parish register of Knebworth in Hertfordshire having the following entry under the year 1600:

Item, to a collection for the burning of the town of Gamlingo in the Countye of Cambridge – 2s.

The other evidence I can offer is slight. Thomas Langdon's maps of 1602 show the village as it was two years almost to the day after the fire. Surprisingly, there are no gaps in the houses shown, no great swathes of unoccupied land left to help one piece together the course of the blaze as it swept through the village. Just about everywhere that there should be houses, houses there are. There are one or two crofts which ought to contain buildings and do not, and one unoccupied house in Church Street labelled 'a cotage decayed'. But there are two important buildings missing. One is the vicarage. I think I may safely say it was destroyed in the fire because in 1601 the archdeacon's visitation book noted that 'the vicaredge is burnt downe', and it cannot be said more clearly than that. The churchwardens were ordered to use a fifth of the profits from the vicarage each year upon 'repaireinge the howse *to the Queenes Instructions* until it be fully repaired'.

The other building, or rather buildings, which ought to appear on these maps and are not shown belonged to Avenel's manor, whose tumbledown manor house and outbuildings had recently been bought by Merton College. The site of the manor is marked correctly as Bury Close, but the close is empty, as indeed every succeeding map of the village shows it to be. Langdon was too good a surveyor to have overlooked an entire manor. Therefore one must assume it was not there. It was not there in 1604 either, when Merton had an inventory made of the goods and chattels of Avenel's manor. The inventory records only cattle, horses, carts and ploughs, with a few agricultural implements thrown in – no mention of household furniture, dairy equipment or brewing vessels. There is nothing to indicate the existence of a manor house at all.

What about the clues provided by surviving buildings? The whole village was surveyed house by house in the 1960s by the Royal Commission on Historical Monuments, and using their findings and some guesswork of my own, I reckon that six buildings plus the church survived both the fire and the centuries that followed. They are: Merton Manor Farm, the Rectory, the Cock, Whitehall, and two others in Church Street.

And that is the sum total of the evidence: the reader must draw his or her own conclusions from it. Here, for what it is worth, is my idea of what may have happened on the dreadful day of April 21 1600.

One of those chill, blustery east winds which often cut across East Anglia in the spring was blowing. The chance spark which began the destruction of Avenel's manor and ultimately of large tracts of the village itself was quickly fanned into a flame by the wind. Nobody afterwards ever knew exactly where the fire started; some said it began in the kitchen, others said in one of the barns. In a matter of minutes the barns and the crumbling manor house were ablaze. Men and women working in the fields were alerted to the danger by plumes of smoke billowing across the rooftops and by the awesome crackle of flames. Drawn to the scene like moths round a candle, the horrified villagers did what they could. Some tried desperately to save horses, pigs and oxen from a scorching death. Others got hold of the long fire-hooks kept in the church and tried to pull the thatch off the nearest cottages in a valiant attempt to stop the fire spreading, but in their hearts they knew the village was at the mercy of the elements. It was hopeless. All they could do was gather their families about them and watch. And pray.

The searing, fearsome wall of flame drove the villagers back, and showers of sparks leapt high in the air every time a beam or a wall fell to the ground. They watched as the entire manor – houses, barns, stables, dovecotes, carts, ploughs and outhouses – was swallowed up by the fire. Soon the sparks filling the air had set light to the nearest cottage and it too was engulfed.

The wind was now gusting the flames towards the very heart of the village. Within an hour the fire had eaten its way westwards through home after home until it was threatening the church itself. But where the road curved to the left the wind blew the sparks across it and onto the defenceless houses and barns on the northern side of the street, and the church escaped. These houses were soon blazing. The blustery gale meant that some houses in the direct line of the fire survived by chance, while others, apparently safe one minute, were consumed the next.

Where the road curved again, to the right this time, the fire spread back to the south side of Church Street, almost incidentally catching the thatch on the vicarage roof with a gust of incendiary sparks. The trail of burning houses, barns, straw stacks and homeless, helpless people had still not satisfied the fire's terrible appetite, but although the frightened villagers did not realise it, the worst was over.

Behind the buildings now ablaze lay open land, the remains of the village green, which would act as a fire-break, and although a few flames and sparks blew across it in search of still more combustible material the danger was slowly passing. As the fire moved up Church Street the first sparks blew onto the houses in Mill Street. Now the

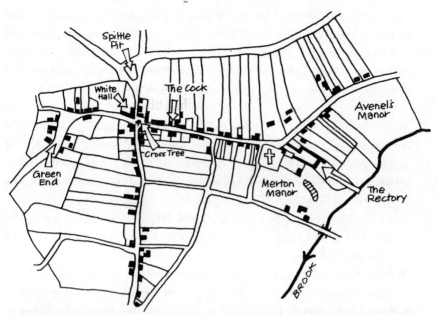

A simplified sketch map of Gamlingay at the end of the Tudor period. It is based on Thomas Langdon's maps of 1602. Although it is only two years after the fire, most of the village has been rebuilt. Note the lack of farm buildings on Avenel's manor.

villagers could see that the fire must soon burn itself out. Since the wind was an easterly and blowing straight across the road, only those at the top end of Mill Street facing the flames suffered. They were the last to go. Beyond them lay open country across which the flames and sparks would not carry. A few hours later only a tree or two was still burning. It was over.

Most of the village was now a smoking, smouldering mess. People gazed in dazed bewilderment at the charred remains of their homes. Gaunt timbers stuck up into the twilight and reminded them that their immediate worry was to find somewhere to sleep for the night. Most of the homeless were able to find a bed with friends or relatives luckier than themselves; others curled up to sleep in a straw-filled barn, or else took refuge in the church.

As they settled down for the night each reflected upon the day's events. For some it seemed like the end of the world, especially the poorer ones, who had lost what little they had. Others, better-off, had lost more in material terms but were already starting to calculate the cost of rebuilding their homes. Someone thought of appealing to the Queen for help, but that would have to wait for another day. Many were just too tired to talk. What little talk there was centred around the amazing fact that not a solitary death had been reported. To most of them, that seemed like a miracle.

Many different versions of what occurred that day could be put forward, but, whether or not my somewhat fanciful account is accurate, the fact is that the after-effects of the fire were not as great as one might think. Langdon's maps illustrate the great speed with which the village was rebuilt in the two years separating the maps from the great event itself. Wealthier villagers took the opportunity to build in a more fashionable, up-to-date way. The fire interrupted the great rebuilding of the village, but also cleared away most of the rickety outdated buildings, enabling better ones to take their place.

The resilience shown by the villagers is remarkable, similar to that following the Black Death 250 years before. In both cases what is impressive is not the devastation suffered but the way the people regained their equilibrium so quickly afterwards. Of course, it may be that due to the paucity of documentation at the turn of the seventeenth century (there are basically only the maps and the Privy Council's letter to go on) I am wrong, and the effects were deeper and longer lasting than I am aware. In reality, though, as with the Black Death, they did not have much choice. What was done could not be undone. Their land was still there, the crops still growing. What was the alternative to rebuilding, and quickly, with or without charitable contributions? The reason that Avenel's manor house and outbuildings were not rebuilt is, as I have pointed out, that they were surplus to requirements once Merton College became the new owners.

On a purely local note there is one further aspect of the fire which needs to be cleared up. Many history books and guidebooks about Cambridgeshire refer to Gamlingay losing its 'important' market to Potton because of this fire, to the great detriment of Gamlingay itself. This is nonsense. The market was never of much economic importance to the village, except perhaps for a year or two back in the thirteenth century when it first started. By 1600 it was ripe for extinction – it had been moribund for most of the previous century. Potton market was a different matter. Ancient and well-established, it did not need the addition of Gamlingay's negligible business to sustain it. The thriving rival market a couple of miles away must have been one of the reasons why Gamlingay's failed.

16

More Court Rolls

I should have liked to be able to talk here about the continuing decline of manorial authority in the village, but none of the court rolls which were undoubtedly kept have survived. From 1511 onwards I am totally in the dark as to everyday manorial life until exactly one hundred years have passed, when two seemingly stray rolls turn up. These are followed by another long gap until 1675, when the series begins again.

The two stray rolls – one dated 1611, the other 1612 – are therefore important. At first glance they are not much different from their predecessors: the eternal list of jurors, essoins and defaulters are all there, although the names are different, naturally. The first roll continues the long-established tradition of restating the by-laws governing the management of the open fields. Here are a few of them, in English for the first time.

Item. for scowringe of ditches that doe disanull the kings majesties high waye, they shalbe scowred by midsomer next, upon the payne of every pole 6d.

Item. hee that hath taken in any Inmate or shall erect any Cottadge shall avoyde them away betwixt this and midsomer next upon payne of fyve pounds.

Item. there is noe man shall take in any stranger but by the consent of the lord and twoe Justices of peece and the sixe men, uppon payne of £5.

Item. noe man shall digg noe turfes but bee turfes, that is turfes for the coveringe of their bee hyves for his owne use, uppon payne of every default 10s.

Item. noe man shall digg noe Claye, nor sand, to make bricke nor tills [tiles] uppon our comon uppon payne of £5 for every default.

There are many more, echoes of similar unheeded instructions from centuries before. This, though, is new:

Item. if the lord and his tennants [farmers of the manor] using the manor or Lordshipp shall keepe them, then wee will keepe all theise orders sett downe; otherwyse wee be att liberty.

This is another way of saying that what is sauce for the goose is sauce for the gander. It is most certainly not the way a jury would have spoken to the lord of the manor even a hundred years earlier. But it would be wrong to assume from this that the court had lost its powers completely, as John Bretherton would have ruefully testified:

Item. wee fynd that John Bretherton hath receyved one William Ierland, beinge a stranger, into this Towne, without consent of the sixe men, contrary to the order therein made; and hath forfyted to the lord £5 for the same.

The 'sixe men' were a sort of reeve committee, supposed to oversee the management of the village land. Fining Bretherton £5 seems rather steep for such a small offence, but there is a simple explanation. The villagers – the tax-paying ones anyway – were afraid that the newcomer and his family would become an extra burden on the new Poor Rate. It is an attitude we shall meet again and again in the coming centuries.

By the time of the court of 1612 these by-laws had been put into effect and the court roll (not surprisingly) consists of dozens of offenders presented for breaking them. Here are some examples:

Item we presente the Widdowe Warrine for keepinge of Catell upon the commone contrarye to the ordares.

Item we presente Thomas Wattares for cuting of Turfes contrarye to the ordere.

Item we present John Hodsonne for takinge In a undersettare In to the towen contrarye to the ordare.

Item we presente Thomas Wattares for diging of claye to macke breckes & tilles upon the commones.

Item we presente Barthallmewe Weebe for taring up of meddowe.

Item we presente Robert Sanforde for In croching upon the hiewaye.

Item we presente John Dent for Diging up the kynges hie waye.

A swingeing attack on the selfish men and women who put their own welfare before the rest of the community? Nothing could be further from the truth. Apart from stating the offence, *no further action was taken* – no fines, no threats, nothing. Perhaps it is not surprising when one takes into account the fact that most of the offenders were jurymen and so sitting in judgement on themselves. As long as they were not involved in any extra taxation most people were prepared to turn a blind eye to anything.

The decline in manorial authority was not as serious as it might have been for the overall welfare of the village because it was a slow process that had been going on for at least 150 years. More importantly it was accompanied by an equivalent rise in the power of the vestry. Rather like a pair of scales, as the manor court slowly descended in prestige that of the parish and its officers slowly rose. But before plunging into the parish records I think it is time we examined Thomas Langdon's maps in a little more detail.

17

The Village, 1602

Merton College paid Thomas Langdon £12 to survey and map their newly-enlarged landholdings in Gamlingay, and the results of his labours with quill-pen and dividers are preserved in the Bodleian Library in Oxford: fifteen priceless documents.

Dated 1602, the documents consist of highly detailed and accurate maps, in colour, of the entire parish except Woodbury (there was no College land there, of course). Langdon's task was to plot the whereabouts of every single strip of land in the parish, and he did it wonderfully well. There is a small-scale general view of the parish showing the woodland, brook, roads, windmills, ancient enclosures and the three great open fields: East, Middle and South. This is followed by larger-scale plans of the village itself, and the individual fields and closes.

On the village plan each house is shown by a tiny sketch of a Tudor building, complete with doors, windows, roof and often a chimney, and labelled with the owner's name and the acreage of the ground it stood on. This is the kind of detail that brings the village to life. It can be seen, for instance, that Christopher Mead lived on the south side of Church Street, with Stephen Hill and Roger Mayes as his neighbours, but if he wanted a drink in Henry Greene's alehouse he would have to walk down the street and past the church to find it. Or if he fancied talking with Isabell Bowers about the incident of twenty years before

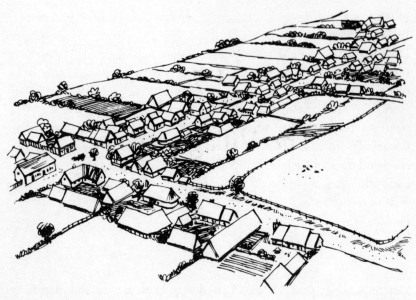

Gamlingay, 1602.

when she was bought by Thomas Upchurche for 16s., he could find her at her cottage standing at the junction of Stocks Lane and Mill Street.

The maps of the fields have the individual strips marked on, with the owner's name and the size of the strip itself written on in an impossibly small script. As a source of field-names alone the maps provide hours of pleasure. Some names are fairly obvious in their meaning, such as Broad Layes, the Sands, Stocking ('field of tree stumps'), West Meadow Banks, Over and Nether Crow Nest, Short-mead, Coney Close, Foxen Furlong and Twelve-acre Piece. Others are less forthcoming, such as Welleses, Cloptons and Maggot's Holme, which took their names from those of their medieval owners. Yet others give a good indication of their use: Broom Close, Walnut Close, Bean Lands, Peasland, Rush Furlong, Willowbed Furlong, Wool Lands and so forth. A few, more ominously, speak volumes about the problems medieval and later farmers faced: Thistle Lands, Water Lands Furlong, Puddle Furlong, Stonehill, Diche Furlong and Clay Croft.

The almost infinite variety of field-names include several which point out prominent village features. 'Monk's Burge' is the name given to the point where a road was crossed by a small stream issuing from what was once the Abbot of Sawtry's estate. Milne Croft, Dovehouse Close and Hatley Hedge Corner need no explanation. I can remember Spittle Pitte – a large pond near the crossroads – and many older villagers still use some of the names mentioned above.

All the major roads are marked as 'ways', usually preceded by the name of the town or village to which they led (you still travel to Cambridge from Gamlingay via Cambridgeway Hill), but the minor lanes and tracks which meandered hither and thither between the fields and furlongs show greater originality in their names. There is a poetic quality to names like Dewberry Heading, Corne Deane, Bennete Hill Haden, Still Deane and Pincott Balke, Snake Hill, Crabtree Haden and 'Pore mannes Lotte'.

Langdon took pride in his skill, as is shown in the way he uses cartouches and heavily ornate scales to embellish the plates. They are not necessary, but they look marvellous. In representing the village as it was in 1602 Langdon was unwittingly looking back across the centuries, because these maps reveal as much about the medieval village as the Elizabethan one. Names and features occurring in thirteenth-century records can, thanks to Langdon, be sited with great accuracy and traced on the ground today. Even where field boundaries have changed, aerial photographs often enable one to plot their original position. Invariably they are exactly where Thomas Langdon said they were.

Gamlingaye towne

Langdon's sketch of the village.

18

Churchwardens

As one would expect, the growing importance of the vestry in village affairs resulted in another tide of documentation. There are church-wardens' accounts, parish registers, constables' accounts, the accounts of the overseers of the poor and a whole host of lesser records, all dating from the seventeenth century and all preserved in the County Record Office in Cambridge, where they can easily be inspected.

For the first half of the century the churchwardens' records are the most revealing. They take the form of annual accounts, made up and audited each year during Easter week or at Whitsun, when fresh churchwardens were elected, and they run, with a few gaps, from 1608 until 1745.

The office of churchwarden is of great antiquity. It was a temporal office, and although the new churchwardens rode off to Cambridge each year to be sworn in by the archdeacon (and duly recorded their expenses in the accounts) he had no power to disallow the appointments. There were normally two churchwardens, and their accounts, although shorter and more straightforward than the earlier bailiffs' accounts, contain a fantastic amount of detail. They were usually written in a flimsy paper booklet or on a single sheet of paper and are very difficult to read. Even when one has unscrambled the inky scrawl one is left with some very idiosyncratic spelling. Ben Jonson's dictum that only a dull man would spell a word the same way twice was taken at face value by the churchwardens. It took me a long time to realise that baggers, bagers, baggets, baggards, bajers, bajuers and bajeers were all not very successful attempts at spelling 'badgers'. But what, you may ask, have badgers to do with churchwardens? The answer to that question lies in an Act of Parliament which made the church-wardens responsible for controlling 'Noyfull Fowles and Vermyn'. The documents are full of entries like these:

paid for a heg hog, 4d.
for tow bagards heds from John Baratt, 2s.
for wone [one] powle Catt head, 4d.
paid to Franice Harvie for toow bageard, 2s.
to John Barret for 4 foxe heades, 4s.
laid out for Caching of sparrowes to Kinge, 2s. 6d.
paid for taking of moles in the Church yard, 3d.

I should love to know what the churchwardens did with all the animal heads that they were presented with, although it is a fair bet that most of the birds ended up in someone's cooking pot.

Parish pest-control officer was just one of the many duties that the churchwardens undertook which appear to have been almost entirely secular. Similarly, during the first forty or fifty years of the seven-teenth century they were to all intents and purposes overseers of the poor. The great Elizabethan Poor Law Acts had laid the foundation of a system of poor relief that lasted for 200 years and more. Very simply, the law said that rogues, vagabonds and 'sturdy beggars' were liable to transportation; strangers settling in a parish were to be removed if they could not furnish security discharging the parish from all expenses likely to occur if they became unemployed; and the indigenous parish poor were to be maintained and set to work by the overseers. Usually the overseers consisted of the churchwardens with one or two substantial householders, who raised the money to relieve the poor by levying a rate.

I shall be able to say more about the poor when we come to look at the overseers' accounts later on, but in the meantime the early churchwardens' accounts give a good idea of the problems involved. These entries, in this case taken from the accounts of Stephen Apthorpe and Thomas Wallis in 1610/11, are absolutely typical:

layed forth to the Criple, 6d.
layed out to the pore man licensed, 2d.
layed forth twoo pore men burnt with fier and had a passe, 4d.
layed forth unto one pore woman that had a passe, 2d.
To one man licensed burnt with fier, 4d.
To one pore man that cam with a passe, 3d.

These people armed with passes, or 'passengers' as they were often known, were licensed to beg on their way to their home parish, where they could expect relief – of a sort. Their first port of call on entering a new parish seems to have been the churchwarden. These licensed beggars became more of a problem as their numbers increased during and after the Civil War, becoming something of a drain on parish resources. I should like to know which of the churchwardens was the 'soft touch' when in 1645/6, at the height of the Civil War, he authorised these payments:

Given a man that hade lost his goods, 1s.
Given to a minister being plundered & in wante, 1s.
Given to a ministeres wife & 4 childirin, 2s.
Given to a woman that hade loste hure meanes, 8d.
Given to anould man by consent of sume of the parish, 2s.
Given to two that had lost thar Estates in Irland, 1s.
Given to a man & wife having many children, being undon by plundering & burning, 2s.
Given to two women that had thare husbandes slayen and having many children, 2s.

This is not the normal hard-hearted, tight-fisted attitude usually found among people whose business it was to dish out money to the poor and needy. The quotations above (and there are many more I could quote) graphically illustrate the effects of the Civil War on the ordinary men and women of England; the darker side of poverty, homelessness and sheer misery are often forgotten by history books. That payment to an old man 'by consent of sume of the parish' is a hint of the tensions that must have existed in Gamlingay, as in the rest of the country, at the time.

In a similar vein, my imagination is fired by bald statements like these:

1624/5

Allso to a man which suffered shipwracke under the Turke, 12d.

1647/8

Paid to 2 men that had bin imprisoned by the Turkes, 6d.

1662/3

Laid out to Robart Morten that wase sold in to Turkey, 1s.

True-life stories of piracy and shipwreck, or sheer blarney? I do not know. Neither, I suspect, did the churchwardens.

Much of the churchwardens' work in relieving poverty was far less romantic. Apart from 'passengers', they were expected to look after their own parish poor, until the job became too big for them to handle and the overseers became a separate entity towards the middle of the seventeenth century. Dealing with the poor was no easy task at the best of times. Many were old and sick, some were young and sick, and quite a few were widows. The cash payments they received (like the 'six pence a weke for 48 wekes' that Widow Catlyn somehow survived on in 1645/6) were unlikely to keep them alive for very long without some form of material help. The accounts are full of items like the 'come of Cooles' (a sack of coal) bought in 1639 for John Paine, or Kate Whalesbie's shoes which cost the churchwardens 2s. in 1623, or the 3s. 4d. 'Leayed out for cloth & making of twoo smockes for widow Hemming' in 1610.

These payments were often made during times of sickness or desperate need, but usually only for a short time. The sick either recovered or died, and the needy found work or, presumably, relieved their own distress. There were a few people permanently 'on the parish', such as Edward Foreman, who was paid amounts varying between 3d. and 1s. a week during 1610/11, or like Widow Catlyn. Their numbers were to grow steadily throughout the century. It was a case of the wealthier villagers either paying up or watching their neighbours starve to death.

Unfortunately for the churchwardens and those who had to meet the rate, the expense did not stop there. Not only was money doled out to keep the sick and needy alive, but there was also the possibility that some sort of medical attention would be required. Most villages had their healers, able to cure many of the ills which beset their patients

– or at least who thought they were able, which does not necessarily amount to the same thing. Goody ('Goodwife') Titmus was one such, as this next entry shows:

1631/2
mor to Goodye Tichmues for healinge of belles leage, 3s. 4d.

I do not know what Bell had done to his leg, but I imagine that Goody Titmus had set it when it was broken; judging from that terse entry it sounds as if her treatment worked. Inevitably, there were times when the treatment was beyond the simple bone-setting accomplishments of village healers and a more expert hand was called in. That same year the churchwardens paid 7s. 6d. to a Mr Jessupe 'for widow Basse and Willyam Baxter, for leten blude & Giveine them visecke'. Bloodletting was, as is well known, for centuries the panacea for nearly all ailments.

The poor who died – killed by the cure, perhaps – were occasionally buried at parish expense, but again we can look at that in more detail when we come to the overseers' accounts. As an aside, I mentioned previously the practice of paying to be buried within the church itself, and the churchwarden's accounts prove that the privilege was still sought after in the seventeenth century. In 1644/5 they received 6s. 8d. (seemingly the standard fee) from Francis Jesop – no relation to the bloodletter so far as I can tell – for 'berring of his father in the church'.

When death did strike there were often orphans to consider. The standard practice was to 'put them out', or in other words to apprentice them to a local man who was supposed to teach them a trade. Then, when the apprentice had served his time, it was hoped that he would be able to make his way in the world without becoming a charge on the parish. Usually the poor orphan was fitted out with a set of new clothes at the start of his apprenticeship as a gesture of goodwill. With luck it would be the last payment he would receive. This next quote, taken from an undated account which from other evidence dates to the early seventeenth century, is typical:

the layengs out
for stuffe for hoose & dublett for Jacksons boy, 3s. 6d.
for one ell of lynne cloathe to lyne his dublett, 14d.
for three els of hempene cloath to make him shirts, 2s. 6d.
for making & washinge them, 6d.
for buttons & threade, 2d.
for making of his two suits, 3s. 4d.
for a hatte, 12d.
for a paire of shooes, 16d.
for a paire of stockings, 20d.
for a knife, 2d.
given to his master with him, 20s.

Many indentures made between master and parish have survived. They set out the terms under which apprentice and master were bound. One example will do for many. In 1645 John Lunn, 'a poore fatherlesse and Motherlesse Childe', was put out to Stephen Apthorpe, 'yoman', until he reached the age of twenty-four (Lunn was about eleven years old at the time), being bound to

faythfullie serve in all such lawfull busines as the said John Lune shalbe putt unto, Accordinge to his power, witt & Abilitie, & honestlie & obedientlie in all things shall behave hymselfe towards his said Master, his wyffe & Children . . .

For his part Apthorpe agreed to teach him the 'crafte, misterie and occupation which he useth in husbandrye' as well as to house the boy and provide him with 'Meate, drinke, lynnen, woollen, hoose, shooes and all other things needfull or meete for An apprentice, Accordinge to the Custome of the Countie of Cambridge'.

Whether things turned out in that way mostly depended on the master. If he was kindly and humane the lad could emerge from a long and happy apprenticeship as a skilled craftsman or husbandman well able to take care of himself. But if the master was harsh and tyrannical the orphan could look forward to a miserable and lonely existence.

Another responsibility that had devolved to the churchwardens was the upkeep of what was called the 'town house', perhaps a throwback to the guild of the Trinity. A brief excursion into the next century tells us what the town house was used for. Richard Apthorpe complained to the Quarter Sessions of 1701 that a House situate near the Church on the High Road leading from Oxford to Cambridge, *wherein the Heardsman for the said Parish usually dwell* is fallen into decay; and that it appearing to this Court that the said Tenement hath been heretofore repaired by the Church Wardens and Overseers and other Inhabitants of Gamlingay, it is ordered by this Court that the Church Wardens and overseers . . . forthwith repair the said Tenement . . .

Several substantial landholders appealed against this decision and won a ruling in their favour that only those people who exercised their common rights should pay for the upkeep of the town house, and definitely *not* the Richard Apthorpes of the village. This reflected the prevalent attitude: why should Richard Apthorpe pay for the town house? It was of no use to him.

The primary function of the churchwardens, however, was to ensure the smooth running of church affairs. In addition to presenting people at the Church courts (as we have already seen) they had to keep the church itself clean and in good repair, see that the fixtures and fittings were properly maintained and look after the churchyard. Their accounts contain hundreds and thousands of items concerning this aspect of their duties. One regular task was providing bread and wine for the Holy Communion:

Layed out at Whitsontide for bred and wine, 2s. 1d.
Layed out for the feching of it, 2d.

In 1610/11, when those payments were made, the churchwardens paid out a total of 25s. 11d. for the bread and wine used at Michaelmas, Christmas, Easter, Maundy Thursday, and what the writer of the accounts called '*Plam* Sunday' and 'Low *Sundunday*'. I think I can guess who finished off the leftover wine!

Another annual expense seems at first glance rather odd:

for karreing of a lode of Rushes to the Church, 8s.
paid to John Basse for feching Rushes for the Church, 1s.

Odd, that is, until it is explained that they were used 'to strewe the churche'. Rushes were spread on the floor at important Church festivals, but usually only beside the pews belonging to the village gentry. The practice seems to have been a purely ceremonial one, and probably dates back to medieval days when there were no pews and the church was strewn with straw or rushes for the congregation to sit on.

Every few years the church interior needed painting. Originally the walls had been covered with pictures illustrating biblical scenes but these were now considered 'Popish' and a coat of whitewash hid them from sensitive Puritan eyes. So one finds, for instance, John Wayman being paid £10 in 1632/3 for 'whitin the Church & mendin the aylles & mendin the flore in the stepel'. What sort of brushes were used to apply the whitewash? Answer: 'a Brush Besume when thay whited the church, 2d'. And how did 'thay' reach the far cobwebby corners? By paying John Overall 2s. 6d. 'for his lader for whiting the Church'.

Times had changed since 'Popish' days. It was no longer necessary for the villagers to tell the time by the crude sundial hacked into the wall on the south side of the chancel, or by the movement of the sun across the heavens. The new clock on the church tower could do the job more accurately and in all weathers, for those who could tell the time. Those who could not, or who dismissed the clock as 'new-fang-led', probably still used the old methods. At any rate the church-wardens seem to have kept the sundial repaired – or, at least, they once paid out 10s. for 'figgering the sun Diall and a Noman', the gnoman being the piece of metal that throws a shadow on the sundial.

The clock needed constant maintenance, and virtually every set of accounts shows money spent on it in one way or another. These are just three examples:

1624/5
paid to the smyth for worke about the clocke and bells, 12d.

1634/5
I laid out for wyere for the Clocke, 2s. 2d.

1639/40
laid out for oyle for the Clocke, 8d.

Sometimes the men who wrote the accounts were as unable to understand mechanical devices as I am. This next quotation, taken from the accounts of 1640/1, is a particular favourite of mine:

Item. paid to James Robardes *for mending sumthing for the Clock*, 2s. 2d.

The clock, patched up and repaired, gave its last tick in 1673, when a new one was bought for £20 which proved almost as troublesome as the old one.

As one would expect, the fabric of the church had money spent on it every year. I can only give a sample from many entries. This is just some of what Thomas Warner and Francis Ratford 'laid out' during 1613/4:

for woode for the Plummer in June 1613, 6d.
for a bushell of malt for Morter, 3s.
for 3 pecks and a halfe of Cinders for morter, 22d.
to the mason for carryeinge in the lyme and helpeing to choose the brick, 6d.
for diggeinge and carryeinge two lodes of Sande, 8d.
for five hundred of Bricke, 7s. 2d.
for mendeinge the greate bell clapper, 5s. 6d.
for mendeinge the clocke hannd, 4d.
for the churchyard gate, 4s.
for two belropes, 5s. 6d.
for three fete of glasse, 18d.

It was endless. If it was not the pulpit door that needed 'one Joyngt' making for it, then they had to pay Leonard Crane for 'making an end of the church wall'. Money had to be spent on 'sawing of bordes & other worke of mending of seates', for '2 lokes for the Church gates' or on 'nedfull ieron worke to trus the bell' and so on. A number of village craftsmen and Jacks-of-all-trades were kept busy by the church-wardens in their worthy efforts to preserve the church (the battle still goes on, of course).

Apart from paying the wages of the smiths, the carpenters, the plumbers and so forth they were also responsible for paying the stipends of the Church officers: the sexton and the parish clerk, and the bellringers, who seem to have had the best deal of all. Guy Fawkes unwittingly provided the bellringers of England with an excuse to demonstrate their skill — as indeed did any other suitable occasion — and the ringers were paid not in cash but, fittingly enough, in ale.

The churchwardens also had to keep in good repair the various items used in the church's services, and repairs and replacements often feature in the accounts. One of the largest outlays came in 1614 when they levied a rate on the parish 'towardes the buyeinge of a greate Bible, The Apologie of the church and other necessarie charges', although in fact they had already bought Bishop Jewel's *Apologies* (a popular defence of the Church of England) and a new bible during the previous year. The bible was without doubt the new Authorised Version of King James. Churchwardens were obliged by law to obtain both books for their church. The combined cost of the two books was £3 14s. 4d.

Also on a royal note, in 1608/9 they paid for making 'the kynges armes & tenne commanddementes' as ordered by the Archdeacon's court, and for 'a tabell for marreges', both of which had to be displayed in the church. The arms of King James in gay colours with the Ten Commandments written below were probably painted on the chancel arch and must have gone some way to brightening up the otherwise plain, whitewashed church.

The churchwardens' accounts abound in fascinating detail, but my space (and my reader's patience) is limited. So too was the church-wardens' income. Usually it consisted of interest ('use' money) on cash lent out, occasional gifts from wealthy men, rent from the church meadow and town house, and what was raised by rate. Frequently this was inadequate to meet all the expenses, and the churchwardens must often have dipped into their own pockets when there was a shortfall. And with this welter of business to attend to, all of it unpaid and part-time, remember, they could be forgiven for heaving a sigh of relief when their year of office came to an end. They must have received some satisfaction from doing a demanding job, but I doubt whether they got more than grudging thanks from the rest of the village for doing it.

19

Nuncupative and Other Wills

Thomas Bowers began his will with the words: 'To all Christian people to whom this present writing shall come, Thomas Bowers sendeth greeting'. Sadly, the rest of his will follows the general trend of seventeenth century wills, which decrease in interest as the century wears on and the disposition of such cash as the testator possesses looms larger than ever in his thoughts. This is not to say that these later documents are devoid of interest. Even the dullest of them may contain a juicy tit-bit, like Elizabeth Johnson's of 1645. She knew that the traditional way to show that a relative had incurred one's wrath was to leave them only a shilling. The trouble with this was that it left future generations guessing as to why it had been done. Widow Johnson was determined that nobody should be in any doubt about why she treated her son-in-law in the traditional manner:

I give and bequeath unto Thomas Warner, the husband of my daughter Elizabeth, deceased, the some of twelve pence to be paid him *upon demand* after my decease; and the reason why I give him noe more is because he hath consumed and spent his owne estate, and my daughters portion, and now lives in an Idle and debayst course of life.

In Gamlingay the early seventeenth century sees a scattering of 'nuncupative' or spoken wills. These often turn out to be the most interesting wills of all. The testator was usually on his death-bed, and had, through carelessness, undue optimism, accident or sheer indecisiveness, neglected to make a will in good time. The witnesses at the bedside later swore on oath a statement recording the dead man's final wishes, and this, in written form, was a legally acceptable will. The resulting documents are, as near as makes no difference, verbatim reports of the dying man's last words.

As an instance of how these wills can take you back three and a half centuries and into the houses of people then living in the village, take that of Henry Harper. On 23 April 1613 he was 'sicke in bodie' and 'sitting by the fire in the house of his Brother William Harper' in Gamlingay, trying to keep warm while the sharp east wind blew outside. Everybody could see that he was extremely ill. His mother, Agnes Steward, with singularly little concern for his health but a great deal of concern for his belongings asked her son Henry 'what he would give her', to which he gratifyingly replied 'she shoulde have five poundes'. Poor Henry's illness, whatever it was, grew rapidly worse, for

the next daie followinge, as he lay in his Bedd in the said house . . . Henry Harper asked if Agnes Wheelewright [Henry's niece] were come home from schoole, and his said Mother sayinge unto him, here she is now, what will thou give her? he said she should have three poundes; and his said Mother demanndinge of him who should have his paire of flaxen sheets and his Coverlett, he said . . . Agnes Wheelerwright should have them.

Perhaps it is just unfortunate phrasing, but it does sound as if the old lady was more concerned about where her son's effects were going to end up than in the fact that he was dying before her very eyes. This impression is strengthened by the calculating way in which she said to him 'that he had given her five poundes, and asked him where she should have it. And he said it was in Squires hande'.

Another Henry, Henry Franklin, provides a further example of those sad people who breathed their last knowing they were leaving defenceless orphans behind. Franklin hoped he was providing adequately for his children when he said Alice Empson 'shold have his goodes and Chattles, and that herewith she shold have a care to bring them up and provide for his children, Elizabeth Franklin, Joan Franklin and William Franklin'.

That was in 1619. Three years later the blacksmith, Zachariah Gray, was equally worried about the fate awaiting his wife and children with the breadwinner gone. He said 'by word of mouth unto his wife Dorothy Gray' that she should have his few belongings 'because his children were all yong, and that she shold have need of it to bring them up, repeating it oftentimes, that all that he had wold not bring his children up'.

By way of contrast, John Martin's nuncupative will made in 1626 contains no such sentiments. He was a labourer and a bachelor, and what little he had was mostly left to his kindred, except for a little cash 'to make a good drinking for such as shold attend him to his buriall'.

Finally, I must record the touching fidelity of George Hayward, grocer, who said 'I do give my wife Fortune all that I have, I will give nothing from her'.

The everyday wills of this period also have their moments. There is the usual crop of revealing preambles. Stephen Apthorpe described himself in 1616 as a 'yeoman, beyng mynded to set a quyet Course betwene my sonnes after my decease', and he was probably correct in thinking there would be friction following his death. As owner of the Cock and much more besides there was a lot at stake. Elizabeth Apthorpe's complaint that she was 'full of panie & misery of my body', and Christopher Dimmocke's hopeful statement that he was only 'somewhat weake in body' deserve mention. So does Christopher Mead, whose will hammers home the point that infant mortality was frighteningly high when he requested burial in the churchyard 'right over against the crosse on the south side, neare to my fathers grave, *above all my children that are already buried*'.

Much else in the wills is the kind of thing we have looked at before. Some men were still trying to force their wives to remain widows by imposing financial restrictions upon them, while others proved more liberal. I shall quote from Robert Bestowe's will (1617) as much for the peaceful bucolic picture it evokes as for its information about male attitudes. He gave his wife Elizabeth:

the little howse which stands in the yarde and . . . my daughter . . . or her husbande shall sett up a chimney therein, and likewise she shall have . . . the grasse plott lyeing next the same, and the little garden plott next to Haywards hedge and abbuttinge against the well, and Comons for a Cowe, if she keepe one.

my said daughter shall have the use of the well, findinge halfe the charges of buckett and rope . . .

my said wife shall repayre the said howse and Leantoe . . .

she shall dwell in my now dwellinge howse till such tyme as the other howse shalbe made ready for her . . .

The great rebuilding has started again, and the village still possesses many examples of seventeenth-century modernisation. Those people who could afford it continued to erect chimneys and ceilings over the old open halls, and live in an altogether more comfortable manner than their forefathers.

Urias King's will, made in 1609, demonstrates some of these improvements, mentioning 'all the pothangers and yron work in the Chymney' – cooking being done on the open fire, with meat roasted on spits in front of it. Some of his food was doubtless cooked in 'the Brasse pott which we use Daiely' and the 'brasse pott with 3 feete', and served on 'the best platter'. Margery Parsons left her grandson 'the standing bedstead, it stands up in the loft'; like many people she now slept upstairs. Beds are still the most important items of furniture and are sometimes said to be 'wherein I lye', although Elizabeth Bestowe's 'matteris which bee upon mee' is a reference unique in these wills. Chairs and tables are normally 'joined' but occasionally trestle tables, survivors from an earlier age, are noted. Chests and coffers are still much in evidence, but Richard Bestowe's 'presse cubbard standing within the parlour' (1640) is an indication of the type of furniture that was slowly replacing chests, coffers and hutches of all descriptions. Dorothy Mause was an old-fashioned lady, relying on the traditional forms of decoration – 'the painted cloth against the wall' and 'the painted dish and the painted cloth that hangeth over the table' – which were medieval in origin, and the gowns, smocks and 'my best ruffe' that she had worn in the far-off days of her youth.

The ruffs so familiar from Tudor portraiture hardly get a mention. By the time they had descended far enough down the social scale to merit distribution in a will of this sort they had gone out of fashion. Other clothing rarely receives more than a passing note, although it is clear that the gorgeous colours and rich materials have gone, replaced by more humble, homespun, dull and altogether more appropriately Puritan clothing. Widows, as before, invariably remember even the smallest item of clothing they possess.

Most of the cloth used to make these clothes was woven in the village. Weaving was a cottage industry, so it comes as something of a surprise to discover that the spinning-wheel, the ancient symbol of the craft, occurs in only two wills. Walter Carton, a labourer, left 'one paire of Stock cards, and one paire of hand-cards, two Linnen wheeles and one woolen wheele'. Joan Huckle left her 'lynnen wheel and a wollen wheel'. The only person to describe himself as a weaver was William Scot, who died in 1630, and left 'a broad lome and two courtell [canvas] flayes', but other people describe themselves as 'shearman' or 'fellmonger', bearing testimony to the importance of cloth in the village. Both shearmen left 'tenters', frames for stretching cloth on, from which the word 'tenterhooks' derives.

As time went on the importance of wills lessened, while the scriveners who wrote them (paid by the line) became more and more verbose. From roughly 1660 onwards there is little of any value in them. As luck would have it, an addition to the wills now often appears, one that is more revealing about houses, less so about individual characters. The wills have told us all they can.

20

The Religious See-saw

Until 1660, England was continually wracked by upheavals of one sort or another: we have seen manifestations of them in the church-wardens' accounts. One imagines the men of Gamlingay agonising over their divided loyalties and arguing among themselves as they tilled the fields – should they support the King or Parliament? That is pure fancy, I am afraid. The whole of eastern England supported Cromwell and his Roundheads. Gamlingay, like so many villages in East Anglia, had ties with the Cromwell family, and like the rest of the area had no choice but to back the parliamentarians. There is no way of knowing how many men from Gamlingay were actively involved with Cromwell's Eastern Association – I have not a scrap of evidence – but I do know that two brave souls, George Fisher and Francis Harvey, joined the cavaliers and were rewarded with a small pension at the Restoration. At a higher social level, Sir John Jacob mortgaged Woodbury manor to raise money for Charles I. But as far as the village documents are concerned the Civil War might never have happened.

It is a different story when it comes to the religious convulsions associated with it, however. The resident clergy in particular suffered some distress. Some of them were of high calibre. James Marsh and John Earle, both rectors of Gamlingay in the 1630s, achieved high ecclesiastical office. Marsh became chancellor and archdeacon of Chi-

chester and Earle chaplain and tutor to Prince Charles, then Bishop of Worcester and Salisbury. Lesser men like John Woolridge (or Worlich) were not so lucky. He was instituted as vicar in 1629, but fell foul of zealous Puritanism, lost his job in 1645 and had to wait until 1662 to get it back. Charles Gibbs, rector from 1637 and a prominent preacher, was forced to give up his living in 1647 and leave the village. But religious fervour was by no means confined to the Puritans. These comments were made by a post-Restoration clerk of the parish on the abilities of his predecessors under the Cromwellian Commonwealth. They are recorded in the Parish Register:

Mr Hills was a woefull bad Register [i.e. Registrar], as he could scarcely spell or write, but he dying in 1655 was succeeded by John Toseland, *equally eminent*.

John Toseland,
'equally eminent'   Ouch!

Once again, the religious see-sawing did its share of damage to the church. In 1638 Matthew Wren, the Bishop of Ely, ordered the churchwardens to 'turne the ministers deske, the seates to be cutt lower'. Six years later William Dowsing, a Cromwellian commissioner from the opposite end of the ecclesiastical spectrum, ordered 'Superstitious Pictures & crosse to be taken downe, which the churchwardens promised to doe'. By 1665 the bishops were back in favour and the churchwardens were told to restore the communion rails (then in the west end of the church) to their proper place.

Although it raised hackles on both sides of the ecclesiastical fence, the damage inflicted on the church was not particularly important in the long run. A much more important result of these upheavals was that many villagers turned away from the established Church, and began to worship in ways more amenable to themselves.

21

Apthorpes

To start with there were four of them, almost certainly brothers:
Walter, William, Richard and Thomas. In the late 1400s they were
known as Aythorpe, which for some reason soon became Apthorpe.
They probably settled first in Woodbury, but soon moved the mile or
so into Gamlingay proper and began to make their mark on the
village. The brothers made constant appearances in the manor court.
Walter was fined twice for assault (once with a pothanger) and
William was fined for fighting with Thomas Langley shortly before,
with unconscious irony, he was elected constable. William was thus
the first in a long line of Apthorpe officials. Richard and Thomas made
more frequent appearances but for more mundane reasons: default,
breaking the Assize of Bread and poaching. Some of their appearances
have already been noted, as has the fact that the court rolls for the
sixteenth century are missing. Had they survived I have no doubt they
would have contained the names of dozens of Apthorpes.

The phenomenon of one family dominating the affairs of a village
is a common one. In Gamlingay the Apthorpes were active for about
300 years, but for most of the sixteenth century they had to be content
to play second fiddle to the Russells, Ratfords, Webbs, Bestowes and
Basses, who ruled the village between them. Then, around 1600, the
Apthorpes emerge as the leading village family, with a finger in just
about every important village pie. Perhaps it had something to do

with the eclipse of the fortunes of the Russell family which occurred at about the same time. It certainly helped that the Apthorpes were such an enormous family, related by complicated means to virtually everyone who mattered, and many who did not.

The seventeenth century saw the ubiquitous Apthorpes reach the height of their power and influence. Before their decline and eventual disappearance in the eighteenth century there were few (if any) village assets which did not sooner or later belong to one of them: land, shops, inns, mills, the larger houses, malthouses and so forth, all became a part of the Apthorpe empire.

The Apthorpes were also inveterate office-holders. It was a rare year when there were no Apthorpe churchwardens, Apthorpe constables or Apthorpe overseers. Their power spread far and wide. There were just so *many* of them: between 1606 and 1749 there were at least seventy-eight Apthorpes born in Gamlingay – probably many more, but the records are incomplete. Many of the male Apthorpes were given the same christian name: Stephen, which is fair enough, I suppose. Lots of Basses were named John, and there were several Thomas Ratfords. But there were at least a dozen Stephen Apthorpes active in seventeenth-century Gamlingay, which causes a certain amount of confusion, especially when one is trying to sort out their family tree. Heaven knows what confusion it caused at the time. (I would like to travel back in time to, say, 1640, then stand in the middle of Church Street and yell 'Stephen Apthorpe' at the top of my voice, just to see how many people answered.) Just to be different, one male was christened 'East' Apthorpe, an example of the mother's surname being used as a Christian name.

Of the many Stephen Apthorpes most were, of necessity, distinguished by epithets, which often serve to illuminate their individual social standing. There was a Stephen Senior and a Stephen Junior, Stephen the Elder and Stephen the Younger. There were Innkeeper and Shopkeeper Stephens, Farmer, Yeoman and Dissenter Stephens, a Stephen 'Gentt' and a Stephen 'of Brook End', although how one knew when a Junior became a Senior, a Younger an Elder or a Yeoman a 'Gentt' is beyond me.

There was even a Grocer Stephen, and he had the distinction of being one of only two people in the village ever to have their own coins made. Actually, they were trade tokens, used during periods when small change was in short supply, and exchangeable only in Grocer Stephen's shop. He had three issues minted: in 1657, 1659 and 1666, all worth a farthing and all bearing the legend 'Stephen Apthorpe of Gamlingay' (or 'Gamlingham', or 'Gamlingam'). The only other person to have these tokens made was Joseph Harvey, also a grocer, who did the same thing in 1667. How did the village support *two* grocers?

Eventually, of course, like all empires, the Apthorpe power waned. One vigorous branch of the family sprang up in Potton. Other branches withered and died, or else moved farther afield. In 1699 Merton manor court could still muster three Stephen Apthorpes, but one was 'of Gransden', a sign of things to come. The last Apthorpe to be buried in the village was Mrs Katherine Apthorpe in 1783, after a long and fruitful life during which she gave birth to twelve children. When the Reverend William Cole visited the parish in the mid-eighteenth century he found several monuments to departed Apthorpes in the church which reveal a darker side to at least one branch of the family. Cole said he could 'make neither Head nor Tail' of one erected by Mrs Nicholas Apthorpe to her son, who died in an asylum. Neither can I. He also quotes this, to her daughter:

Here lyeth Rebecca Apthorp, Daughter of Nicholas Apthorp, died Octob: 22 1741; aged 27 yrs.

> Her lies the virtuous pious Maid,
> Who thought herself in Love betray'd;
> Her carnal Mind was first so odd,
> She fear'd thereby displeased God;
> Submitted under Pennance Rod,
> Beyond its Rules for want of Sence,
> Abstained, starv'd herself, from hence.
> A Church of England Member died,
> On Christ her Saviour she relied.
> Her Soul does now with Angels fix,
> With interferring Kisses mix,
> In greater Pomp than Coach and Six.
> No room for Mother's Tears below,
> Who's sure to meet when Trump does blow.

Mrs Apthorpe was described by Cole as 'a Roman Catholic and a little out of the way'. She said her daughter 'A Church of England Member died'. Was there some friction about religion between mother and daughter? Could it be that Rebecca suffered from anorexia nervosa as a result of feeling 'in Love betray'd'? Or was she, like her brother, a victim of the family's mental instability? Or indeed a combination of all three?

I am also intrigued by these references from the overseers' accounts:

1729
Spent when I mett about Ed. Apthorp, 3s. 6d.

1730
to John Parson for Ed. Apthorpe, 14s. 6d.
to Richard Richardson for Looking after Ned Apthorp, 9s.
to Rich. Richardson on Edward Apthorp account £1 17s. 2d.
Spent when we mett about Edward Apthorp to gett him a way, 2s.

1731
to Richard Richardson for Edward Apthorp Chargis att London, £2 2s. 0d.

Richard Richardson was innkeeper at the Castle, and Edward Apthorpe obviously lodged with him. My suspicion that Edward Apthorpe was another of the family in 'want of Sence' is strengthened by the fact that the overseers bought him a large round cheese to eat on nine separate occasions during September 1730 before sending him away to London. It is confirmed by the last entry concerning this poor, tortured man. This comes from the parish register, which duly records that on 12 January 1734 they laid to rest Edward Apthorpe, 'lunatick'.

But the Apthorpes deserve to be remembered for more than the madness which afflicted some of them. They were a vigorous family who in one way or another contributed enormously to the village. They will make many more appearances in this book before they eventually fade out of sight.

22

Goods and Chattels

Theoretically it was only possible for probate to be granted on a will if it was accompanied by a list and valuation of the deceased person's goods and chattels, known as an inventory. The reason for this practice is obscure. It was introduced in the sixteenth century and probably had something to do with the collection of dues in one form or another. The inventory was supposed to be drawn up by two honest, literate men of the village, but this was often easier said than done. Illiteracy is doubtless the reason why one seldom finds many inventories dating from before the mid-seventeenth century, at least outside the towns. Not a single one exists for Gamlingay before 1690. From 1690 until 1781 there are forty-seven in all, now kept in the Cambridge University Library along with the accompanying wills.

From one point of view, inventories are unreliable documents: the valuations given by the two appraisers often bear no resemblance to reality, usually being far too low. Factors of class and personal taste come into the reckoning. So too does the possibility that when an appraiser came to put a value on a cart or a plough or a set of chairs, he had at the back of his mind the thought: 'am I likely to be buying them in the near future?'.

The inventory normally begins with a brief statement. This one is typical of them all:

A true And parfet Invinetare of the Good And Chatells of Edward Bass of Gamlingay in the Countey of Cambridg, bacholder, Deceseed, Aprased And vallud as foleth by us, howe names is under Riten, this fust day of may 1690.

The word 'inventory' caused the appraisers endless trouble; one anonymous appraiser said that he was writing an 'Imnaritary' of James Wells's goods. However, Nicholas Paine, who really ought to have known better, and Joseph Wilson, who probably did, deserve some sort of posthumous recognition for rendering 'kitchen' as 'Chiching'.

One common feature of the documents is the annoying tendency of the appraisers to lump together all the smaller items of furniture in a room under the all-purpose heading 'other lumber'. Once the appraisers even went so far as to add 10s. to an inventory for 'Lumber and *things not seen*', which begs the question, how do you value something you have not even seen? It is a good illustration of what I mean about taking the prices given in the inventories with a pinch of salt.

Often, but by no means always, clothes are put first on the list, together with any cash the appraisers found when sifting through them (hence the need for honesty as well as literacy). Disappointingly the simple phrase 'wearing apparell and money in his/her purse' is the nearest we get to a description of the clothing. The combined valuation of the clothes and the cash ranges from a few pounds in most cases to a few shillings in some. It was largely a fictitious sum in any case, a round-figure approximation not meant to be taken too seriously. For example, at his death in 1731 Thomas Cawthorne had 'His Waring Apparill and one half penny in Purse', which was valued at £4 exactly. Are we really supposed to believe that Cawthorne's clothing was worth £3 19s. 11½d.?

This does not mean that the appraisers were unable to produce a fairly detailed list, and one that could be relied upon to be accurate as far as it went, because they did. When we are told that John Careless had three tables, eight chairs and some pewter dishes in his kitchen, we may be sure that this is exactly what he did have – plus some 'other old Lumber' – but we may safely doubt the price of 15s. that his appraisers put upon it. Most inventories take one on a room-by-room guided tour of the deceased's house and yard as it appeared a day or two after his or her death, and they abound in detail about the house and its contents. This tour usually starts with the downstairs rooms.

Although it was rapidly going out of fashion by being divided up and partitioned off, the hall manages to make an appearance in nine of the forty-seven inventories. By now the word had lost its original meaning and in every case the hall had long since been ceilinged over, and the room or rooms over it called 'hall chamber' or 'chamber over the hall'. The hall by now is just an anachronistic name for what has become an ordinary downstairs room, but one nevertheless with a certain residual prestige often attached to it. John Basse's hall included 'one Dresser, 2 Ovall Tables; shelves and Pewter upon them, 6 Chaires' among 'other Lumber' in 1717, and was obviously his best room. The same is true of Lawrence Mead in 1734, whose inventory goes into greater detail about the contents of his hall:

A Clock, a dreser, ten pewter dishes, thirty pewter plates, a warming pan, a brass kettle, pothook, shovell, tongs, Gridiron, a Jack, a Spitt, a fender, twelve Candlesticks, twelve chairs, two tables, two joynt stools, a boxiron and some earthen ware.

Clocks became modish in the early eighteenth century, as did the looking-glass. The earliest mention of a clock comes in 1711, when Nicholas Apthorpe (who could well afford it) had one 'in the Staircase' of his house in Brook End, but gradually the idea spread among lesser mortals and after 1730 they became commonplace. Indeed, in the fifteen inventories from 1733 until 1781 only four do *not* mention a clock. Nicholas Apthorpe's clock was valued at 25s. How much would one of those 'commonplace' clocks fetch at auction today? Nicholas Fickis had a clock in his hall in 1733, but the picture of genteel cultivation is partially spoiled by the fact that he found it necessary to keep his bacon-rack in the same room.

Art and culture have never played much of a part in the lives of Gamlingay people at any stage in their history (with one or two exceptions) so it is not surprising to find only one example of anybody having pictures in their possession. This comes from Thomas Cawthorne's inventory of 1731, and if his 'Six Picktures and Seven Chairs' are anything to go by, Cawthorne was a hempdresser of aesthetic sensibility. Those pictures arouse my interest: what was the subject matter? Who painted them? Even more interestingly, what happened to them? They were valued, pictures and chairs together, at only 6s., so perhaps one ought to think of the pictures as being not so much exquisite eighteenth-century oil-paintings as cheap prints, similar to the seven recorded in Lawrence Mead's parlour. But how could semi-literate villagers put a value on pictures, whether paintings or prints? Thomas Cawthorne may have had half a dozen genuine Rembrandts hanging on his wall for all the appraisers knew.

Literature fares equally badly. From John de Senkeworth's 'two books of romance' in 1314 until the inventory of John Custerton in 1736 nobody, so far as documentary evidence goes, kept, looked at or read anything more stimulating than an account book. Even Custerton's tomes were lumped together as 'a parcel of Books' worth 10s. Eleven years later Simon Page, cordwainer, had 'some Books', but that dismissive phrase seems to be the limit of anyone's interest in the written word. I would love to know with what literary companions a yeoman and a cordwainer whiled away the long winter evenings.

Returning to the house itself, it seems that the parlour was the second-best room in those houses which had halls, and the best in those that did not. Francis Bacon, a blacksmith who died in 1700, had the only 'Liverey Cupboard' mentioned in these inventories. He stood it in the parlour. Livery cupboards were used not for keeping clothes in but for storing food. Stephen Apthorpe ('Gentt') had 'in the parllor, two tabells, A Clock, Eight Kaine Chaiers, two plaine Chaiers, bellowes, Gratt and other fier Iorns, Candelstick and warming pan' in 1720, which is what one would expect a retired well-to-do gentleman to have in his parlour. What one would not expect – or at least, what I did not expect – was that parlours would continue to be used for the old-fashioned purpose of downstairs bedrooms, but the inventories provide ample evidence that they were. Richard Collins had, for instance:

in the parlor 2 Bedsteads, 2 featherbeads, 2 feather bolsters With Curtaines and vallants and Ruggs and other things there unto belonging; and 2 tables and 3 Turky Worke Cheares With other things, £6 10s.0d.

If I tell you that his cellar contained '4 hogsheads emty and on full on' and that a hogshead was a barrel holding six gallons of beer, you

Richard Collins's Rose and Crown today

would probably guess that Richard Collins was an innkeeper. He owned the Rose and Crown in Dutter End, which is still there, much altered. The brew-house, which in 1692 contained 'a Brass Copper and a Mashinge fatt and all other Brueing vessels', is now a garage. The gatehouse, with its 'little Lodging Roome' nearby has long since vanished. In later years the inn became 'Kitchen's farm', and the house is still sometimes referred to by that name.

The practice of keeping beds in the parlour continued well into the next century. The last inventory, from 1781, has 'In the parler 1 Bed', indicating how conservative even a man like Thomas Main, worth almost £350, could be.

One other downstairs room deserves mention: the kitchen. The rickety lean-to of earlier times had developed into the more familiar 'farmhouse kitchen', an integral part of the structure of a house. Perhaps I should not tell you that Clement Sell kept his 'pewter Chamber pott' in his kitchen, but Robert Adams's 'two flitches of Bacon' was a sight that would have greeted one in most country kitchens until fairly recently. Aptly enough, Francis Bacon had a flitch of bacon as well as 'seven bushills of Wheat' in his. Thomas Nevill's kitchen included one 'tankard, one morter and pestill'. John Webb (yeoman) kept his clock among the fire-irons, pewter dishes, bellows and the obligatory 'other Lumber' of his kitchen in 1712. I doubt, however, if Nicholas Brotherton had room for a clock in his, since it was already overflowing with:

One Jack and three Spitts, two Dripin pans, Hand-irons and fire Shovll and tongs, and the back-iron and pott hoockes, six Peuter Dishes and one flagon and other small peuter; two boylers, four kettles and two skilets, one table and form, six Chairs and other small things, £5 10s. 0d.

Think of that list in terms of actually producing food and you begin to have some idea of the never-ending hard grinding work that housewives had to do.

Most of the larger houses brewed their own ale, and this too was often the housewife's responsibility. The buttery contained the brewing vessels. Not all inventories are as unhelpful as Thomas Atkinson's 'in the butry, all the Bras & Puter'; for instance, the blacksmith Francis Bacon had in his:

three Barrills, two drink stalls, one dow-stant and other small things.

One assumes that while Francis was busy working up a thirst over his forge his wife was engaged in providing him with the means to quench it.

As well as brewing, the housewife had to be something of a dairymaid as well, because the dairy features even more often than the buttery. Nicholas Brotherton's wife must often have busied herself with the 'Cheespress and cheese Tube and one churm and other milk vesells', producing cheese and butter for household use as women like her had done in the village for hundreds of years – likewise Mrs John Basse (1717) with her 'Chesepress, one stand, shelves, Dairy Vessels', and so forth. Most housewives would have baked, although the bakehouse as a separate room does not appear very often. When it does it typically contains 'one Copper, one frying Pan, one dough stand, 5 Tubs, 5 Brass kettles, one Boyler', to stay with John Basse's inventory for a moment.

After listing the items of interest to be seen downstairs the appraisers usually take the reader upstairs and into the bedrooms. Most of them were bedrooms, too, despite being called anything but – 'chamber over the hall', or 'parlour chamber' or 'chamber over the kitchen', but never just a straightforward 'bedroom'. The majority of folk now had beds upstairs. These were the contents of Lawrence Mead's 'hall chamber' (1734):

Mrs Brotherton and servant hard at work in the dairy.

Bedstead, feather bed, Curtains and other appurtenances, £2 10s. 0d.

Chest of drawers, looking glass, a Great chest, hutch, hanging press, nest of drawers, close stool, five chairs, Truckle bed, flock and other appurtenances, £2 1s. 0d.

Twenty pair of sheets, five large table cloths, a dozen of napkins, ten pair of pillowbers and five Towells, £11 0s. 0d.

Much is worthy of note here. The curtains are of the type drawn around four-poster beds, and not window curtains, which are specifically singled out in only two inventories. The hanging press was a wardrobe; the close-stool a descendant of the Tudor 'chair of easement' – a commode. Truckle beds and hutches have been mentioned before, but it is interesting to note their use at such a late date.

Where servants had their own bedroom it normally had little in it beyond the 'one feather Bed, one flock bed, one Cofer, Beding and other Lumber' that John Basse allowed in his servant's room, or the feather bed and two coffers in his maid's room. Servants were there to work, not to laze around in a comfortable room. Mind you, Basse could well afford a 'Maid's Chamber' and the maid who slept in it. His is the only inventory to mention jewellery: three silver spoons and three gold rings kept in the 'Chester drawers' in his chamber over the hall. William Jeakins had the only other silver noted, a 'silver Can'.

Beds are not usually described in any great detail, and other bed furniture is dealt with equally tersely, like the 'curtens and vallens and other beding' of Edward Green in 1693. Not all beds were comfortable four-posters, however. Samuel Lewis was sleeping on 'one straw bedd' in 1726. Compared to him Thomas Cawthorne lay in the very lap of luxury on a bed with a 'Top peice & head Peice & Coard & Curttin Rods' worth 7s. in the opinion of his appraisers. A warming-pan was a very necessary piece of equipment in the days before hot-water bottles and electric blankets, and it finds its way into the inventories as often as it must have been inserted in its owners' beds on cold winter nights.

Clothes, and especially the household linen, were kept upstairs. I find the enormous quantities involved, especially of linen, rather puzzling. Lawrence Mead's twenty sheets and five large table-cloths already quoted are perhaps permissible, but John Basse's forty pairs of sheets, forty-eight napkins, four table-cloths and twelve pillow-cases seems excessive, even for him. And while on the subject I had better note the only reference to a spinning-wheel in the inventories – the 'One Linnen Weel' Elizabeth Skillins kept in 'ye other Chamber'. Alongside it was a cradle, a box, a wheelbarrow, two 'Borkitts' (buckets), a chaff sieve, two ladders, a scythe and a couple of forks, from which I would guess that the spinning-wheel never again saw the light of day. Still, old Mrs Skillins kept some 'wooll & hopps' beside her bed, so anything is possible.

Upstairs rooms had other uses. Most of the larger farmhouses had a cheese chamber, containing, like John Webb's in 1712, 'some Shelves and about seventy Cheeses'. He also had 'sum Aples' in his 'old Chamber'. The smell of cheese and apples wafting through the house must have been mouthwatering. Nicholas Apthorpe stored his apples and cheese in the same room, while one of William Jeakins's bedrooms was home to '11 quarters Malt & skreen, 1 bushel & 3 shovills'. He was a maltster, and the screen and shovels were part of his equipment for making malt from barley. The strain on the floorboards from all that malt must have been immense. A quarter of malt weighed 336 pounds, so Jeakins had nearly one and three quarter tons of the stuff in his malt chamber. The bedroom floorboards of old houses sometimes contain their own evidence of their earlier use; one often finds chaff, pips and so forth lying between and beneath them.

Tools, implements and stock of various trades appear in the inventories when the appraisers had finished in the house and taken their pens and paper into the yard and outbuildings. John Shipston and Stephen Norman could hardly have avoided the 'Ten thousand of bricks' or the mound of 'Brick earth dugg' they found in the yard of Nicholas Fickis, described as a bricklayer, but who must have made his own bricks too. Thomas Atkinson was the village glazier, whose workshop in 1719 was disappointingly dismissed as having 'his Worcking tools, Glase & Lead and other ode things' in it. A rather more complete picture of a workshop comes from John Manton's inventory, 'Taken, Done, and Appraised' in 1752. His workshop was a smithy:

In ye Shop
Three anvills, Three Pair Bellowes, Two Pecking Irons, One Nail Tool, £13.

Three Vices, Files, Hammers and seven Plates, £4.

Two Coal Troughs, and other things belonging to ye Forges, £1.

Two Grindstones and Setts; Chesell, and other tools in ye shop, £2 5s. 0d.

New Iron unwrought, £3 10s. 0d.

New Tire nails and shares and other new Goods made up in ye shop, £8 3s. 6d.

Old Iron, £4.

Spade trees, Snathes, Fork stales [handles], scythes, £2 15s. 4d.

One Brake, a Ladle and some other Farrier's materials, 10s. 6d.

Thomas Cawthorne, whose inventory has already been widely quoted in this chapter, obviously used his 'Pare of Stillyards' and his 'Pare of Scales & Leaden waits' and the 'six Pounds of Six Penny Hemp and a Parcel of Rough Hemp' in carrying on his stated trade of hemp-dresser. Three men earned their living as cordwainers; here is the working stock of one of them – James Meeks, in 1752:

Upstairs.
Twelve small Calf skinns, Two and Twenty Larger Calf Skinns, five Hydes, six Brooken Hydes and Old Pieces, £16 5s. 0d.

In the Shop.
A parcel of Nails, 7s. 6d.
Three Sides of Back Leather, £2 10s. 0d.
A Pair of Boot trees, Three seats, A dozen of Lasts and other Lumber, 15s.
Book debts, £3 10s. 0d.

Book debts and other debts often account for a hefty slice of a man's total wealth, especially a tradesman. Thomas Clarke was owed £25 at his death in 1691, which was almost exactly half of his total worth. John Parsons was due £60 out of the £73 7s. 6d. that the appraisers considered his goods were worth. Thomas Handley, a carpenter, was owed the astonishing sum of £150 out of a grand total of £168 11s. 6d. This is almost certainly due to the practice tradesmen had of sending in their accounts only once a year.

Sometimes, when a man had retired from his working life he lent out his capital and lived on the interest – the very definition of a gentleman. Stephen Apthorpe 'Gentt' was worth £449, but of that sum £400 was due from John Brown of Royston and £20 from Jonathon Phillipes of Gamlingay. It was just about the only way anyone could borrow money before the rise of the country banks displaced the private lender. Even Clement Sell, 'singleman', whose belongings were worth a mere £6 or so, had £65 'out upon bond'.

Ideas and attitudes changed slowly in the countryside. There is really no difference between the medieval villager's contempt for the state of the village roads and that of William Jeakins, three or four hundred years later, whose appraisers noted 'In the Streett, 6 timber sticks'. These 'sticks' were probably large beams lying in wait for someone to fall over in the dark.

The yards and outbuildings were duly visited by the appraisers, but the equipment listed reveals little that is new. Agriculture was much the same as it had been in 1279, with much the same crops being grown and much the same livestock kept.

Nicholas Apthorpe was by far the richest of all the people who left inventories. He was worth £814; the next wealthiest was John Basse, valued at £512. The average value of the forty-seven inventories is £125. Towards the bottom of the list, but by no means really poor, were those people who were worth minute sums. The real poor did not make wills or have inventories made. I have already mentioned Samuel Lewis and his straw bed. Discounting the debts of £35 owed to him, Lewis's worldly goods totalled £3 16s. 0d., and he lived in a one-up, one-down cottage. Equally, John Webb (1727), a shepherd, had only his clothes, a cow, a pig, ten sheep and two and a half acres of land along with a few chairs, a table and two beds. The most forlorn inventory of all is the last one I shall quote and the only one to be quoted in full: ·

Edward Bass, 1690
in primis his waren Aparell And mony in his purse, £5.
on fetherbed, £1 10s. 0d.
six shep, £1 10s. 0d.
in Debetes Despret, £2 0s. 0d.

Stephen Apthorp
the mark of Richard bass

23

Cow-jobbers and the Gingerbread Man

The wills and inventories give a good idea of the trades and occupations of the villagers, or at least the ones who made wills: the bakers, yeomen, husbandmen, carpenters, blacksmiths, innkeepers and so on. More can be discovered from the parish registers.

At various times Gamlingay boasted apothecaries, doctors, a surgeon and assorted midwives. There was a clockmaker, chimneysweep and chapman, as well as tinkers, tailors, soldiers – alas, no sailors – but undoubtedly rich men, poor men, beggarmen and thieves. There was a jockey, a sack-carrier, masons, cow-jobbers and hog-jobbers. There was a brazier, a drummer and a fiddler, woodwards, gamekeepers, grooms, gardeners, haywards and a tilemaker. More exotically, one man was described as a 'Gingerbread man', and another as an 'Oatmeal Man'. Also in unusual occupations were the sievebottomer, the hair-buyer (who presumably sold it to the periwigmaker), the hawker, higgler and numerous pedlars – all following similar occupations – the lacemakers (lacemaking was an important cottage industry in the nineteenth century), the breeches-maker, ropemaker and mat-maker. If you wanted a razor sharpened you took it to the razor grinder; if you were troubled by vermin you consulted the molecatcher or the ratcatcher, depending on which pest you wanted exterminated. And if you were in a different sort of trouble you steered well clear of the excise officer and the chief constable.

The parish registers and their nonconformist counterpart, the Gamlingay Baptist Church minute book, also open up an area that has hitherto been closed. They sometimes tell you the way in which people died. The luckier ones lived their threescore years and ten and died peacefully in their sleep. But with the average life expectancy at around thirty-five years in 1700, death stalked the unwary in a way difficult to understand nowadays, with all the advances in medicine that keep us alive in circumstances which would probably have killed our ancestors. The plague fortunately no longer constituted a serious threat after the middle of the seventeenth century, but almost equally dangerous and much more common was smallpox, which during one outbreak between February and June 1777 killed twenty-three people in Gamlingay.

I offer the following without comment:

Parish Registers

1719
Timothy Norman: 'hanged himself in his barn & was found by jury & coroner to be lunatick'.

1720
'A certain beggar man was found dead Feb 10 under Kipps Hedges'.

1729
John Basse: 'killed by a waggon wheel falling upon him'.

1767
Edward Wooton: 'killed at Waresley with a cart'.

1767
Ann Marriot: 'drowned herself in the well'.

1782
David Dunton: 'killed by overthrowing a cart at the Buts'.

1788
Thomas Stocker: 'the cause of his death was by fighting with young Grocier Jeakings at the Green Man'.

1793
Charles Royston: 'killed at Gamlingay by jumping his mare over a hedge & was taken up dead'.

Baptist Church Minute Book

1722

Susan Webb: 'Left this world after a Long and Lingering disease in a Consumption of Body'.

1723

Thomas Yarrow: 'after he had gone through great pains of the Cholick and a fever attending of the same'.

1729

Elizabeth Ladson: 'departed this Life after a Long and tedious sickness of the Jaundes, and other distempers'.

1732

Mary Squire: 'dying of an Appleplex'.

1796

Nicholas Paine: 'afflicted with a complication of bodily disorders . . . seized with an inflamation in his lungs . . . terminated in his death'.

1798

Mary Charter: 'after a long affliction of the Dropsy'.

24

The Downings

It is time for another look at manorial history.

Returning to the year 1600, Merton College had just purchased Avenel's manor and made itself master of a large proportion of village land. In terms of ownership nothing changes from now on. The College continued to lease its land and farms, and the income continued to disappear into the College purse. In reality its role as lord of the manor was over by the end of the seventeenth century, even though it remained lord of the manor in title for many years to come. The College still tried to behave as though nothing had changed since the Middle Ages, but its inconsequential efforts at trying to influence village affairs through the manor courts proved that the opposite was true.

In 1675 the flow of court records begins again, but these are very different from the earlier records, and by and large not nearly so interesting. That of 1675 is a case in point, repeating the village by-laws *ad nauseam* for the villagers to ignore. Usually the rolls confined themselves to lists of land and house transfers which are of interest to me but not relevant here. Soon, however, the court began to make the threatening noises of old:

wee present that the common pound is out of repere & that the Lords of this Mannor ought to repere the same; & wee humbly pray that it may bee repered by December the 25th next.

wee present Thomas Tomlin for breaking open the pound & takeing out 2 horses, & amerce him 3s. 4d.

wee present Francis Bacon, Thomas Heywood, John Basse, William Lune & Robert Webb for not scouring the ditch at the end of everyone of their closes next great heath; & wee give them time to scoure it till the 28th of November next upon paine of 3s. 4d.

wee present Thomas Witt for digging & carryeing sande from little Heath, & allso wee present him for carryeinge turves from Great Heath, & amerce him 6s. 8d.

wee present all that made default at this Court, & amerce them 4d. apeece.

Nobody could say that the jury didn't try to maintain manorial discipline. On the other hand, nobody could say it succeeded. It is worth noting that the jury now finds itself able to instruct the College, however 'humbly', to carry out what the jury feels are the College's responsibilities. This new-found freedom was carried to extreme by May Fisher:

we present that May the wife of George Fisher hath severall times since the last Court stood in the felds & in other places in the comon feilds within this Mannor & hath *received toll* for severall droves of catle which have passed through the comon, which is an incroachment upon the Lord of this Mannor, & therefore she is amerced 3s. 4d.

The College had long exercised its own ancient and well-defined right to levy a toll when droves of cattle on their way to market passed through the village. Things had changed so much that May Fisher, without right or reason, was demanding the toll instead. She must have been a formidable lady to have forced the tough old drovers to pay up. The College officers knew there was little they could do to prevent her. You may be sure May Fisher did not hand over the 3s. 4d. People with that sort of cheek were not going to be intimidated by an outmoded institution like a manor court. And although I cannot prove any link between her and those fifteenth-century Fishers, it is odd how anyone with the name of Fisher usually meant trouble for the court.

The threats and fines were not quite the last kick of a dying institution. At the turn of the eighteenth century the court baron of

Merton fined a grand total of eighteen people for offences which included 'moweing of fussens one the Common', 'Diging of turfe on the Common', 'Plowing on the Common' and so forth, but the 3s. 4d.s remained unpaid and the College seems finally to have accepted the situation. The courts became purely administrative, concerning themselves with collecting rents and admission fines while leaving the control of recalcitrant villagers to others. This continued to be the case for a long, long time. It was well into the twentieth century before Parliament finally got around to bringing a formal end to manor courts, lords of the manor and nearly a thousand years of history. And with the College's realisation that economic and social changes had curtailed their power and influence, our interest in the courts and their business also comes to an end.

Turning to Woodbury, we left the manor in 1600 in the hands of John Manchell of Hackney, and he left it – heavily mortgaged – to his grandson John. Sometime before 1640 Sir John Jacob (whose star was rising) bought it, and soon after, as I have mentioned before, he was obliged to mortgage the estate to his kinsman, Robert Jacob, in order to raise money for Charles I.

Sir John Jacob financed one of the most impressive buildings in the village: the almshouses. After all the wrangling and jerry-building which had bedevilled earlier attempts, a terrace of ten tenements was finally built in 1665 on a site given by Abraham Jacob in 1628. A tablet was placed in the centre of the row noting the date and the name of Sir John Jacob, a permanent reminder of his generosity. The Reverend William Cole, who visited the parish a hundred years after they were built, said, 'about a Furlong from the Church stands a very handsome Range of Alms Houses of brick, very regular & of two Stories, with an high Wall before them', a description which, like the almshouses, still stands today.

Woodbury was by now in the hands of Robert Jacob. Luckily, a stray document survives which gives one a glimpse of the estate in 1672. The 'mantion house', farms and land were all leased for £506 10s. od. a year, with a further £124 coming from, as the writer puts it, 'severall houses & land in & about Gamlingay towne, lett to severall townes men, I thinke' – an allusion to the financial mess left by earlier owners. Likewise this reference to the park:

There is a parke, well stored with deare, wherof the land & timber is worth about £3,300, but is seazed uppon by one Hancock, a Creditor of Sir John Jacobs, & I know not who hath power to sell it, but it lyes within two or three fliteshots of the mantion house . . .

The manor could be let for £600 a year, said the writer, 'if troubles were not uppon the land', and added that 'a little before Christmas last Sir John Jacob was offered for it £10,000 . . . but the stoppage in the Exchequer hindred the purchasers proceedings'. The 'stoppage in the Exchequer' refers to state bankruptcy; Sir John Jacob's finances were not the only ones in a mess.

Shortly after this rental was made the estate was finally sold, to William Mainstone, an East India merchant, passing to his nephew John Mainstone, who sold it in turn to Ralph Lane in 1696. The estate was groaning under the weight of heavy debts. Lane was a merchant who traded with Turkey, but he did not buy the whole estate. The northern section was sold off separately, causing the isolation of the original manor house. When Ralph Lane died the failure of male heirs meant that the estate followed his eldest daughter into the welcoming arms of George, earl of Macclesfield, and his family. And that is where both she and it must stay for the time being. Our attention now turns to what, for a short period, becomes the most interesting of all these estates: Shackledon.

The Burgoyne family who owned Shackledon in 1600 eventually sold it to Sir George Downing. Downing was one of the best-known and most influential men of his time, reputedly both the richest and the meanest. His name became a byword for miserly selfishness. He managed the difficult feat of serving both Cromwell and Charles II equally successfully, enriching himself at their expense with a laudable lack of political bias. Downing Street in London takes its name from his property there, but perhaps his greatest service to posterity was in employing Samuel Pepys at the start of the diarist's long career in the Civil Service. Pepys found Downing a 'niggardly fellow' and a 'mighty talker', and tells several amusing stories at Downing's expense. But, interesting character though he is, the first Sir George is of little importance to Gamlingay. Much more important is the fact that his grandson inherited his estates – including Shackledon – as well as his grandfather's christian name and title.

This Sir George Downing is another of those Gamlingay men I should like to have met: not for reasons of charm or personality, but because I would like to confirm my feeling that all his life he must have carried with him an indelible air of tragedy. He was born around 1685. and lost his mother a few years later. His father was said to be 'of unsound mind' and young George was brought up by his uncle Sir William Forester. Forester, with both eyes firmly fixed on the Downing fortune, had the lad secretly married to his daughter Mary. He was fifteen, she was two years younger. For reasons that can easily be guessed, young Downing was immediately sent away to school, then, when he was seventeen, he left England on a 'grand tour' of the continent and did not return again for three years. When he did he refused to live with or acknowledge the wife arranged for him by his greedy uncle. She petitioned the House of Lords for a divorce (an Act of Parliament was required) on the grounds of the respective age of the partners at marriage, and Downing supported the petition. It narrowly failed. Thereafter they lived separate lives.

Downing was MP for Dunwich in Suffolk from 1710 until 1715 (the year the divorce failed), then from 1722 for the rest of his life. For all the expense and trouble it took he was never a very active politician, being content to vote with the Whigs. His father died in 1711 and he inherited the Downing estates, then standing at some 7,000 acres. Most of them lay in Cambridgeshire, round Tadlow, Croydon and Bottisham. But it was neither his marital problems nor his politics that left a mark on Gamlingay: it was his decision on inheriting the baronetcy to knock down the family mansion in East Hatley and build a new one on the Shackledon estate that had the greatest effect.

With typical Downing prudence (something else he had inherited from his grandfather) the new mansion was built in part with material recovered from the demolished house in East Hatley. Even so it cost him £9,000. It was a fine building, judging from the estate plan and small vignette of the house preserved in Downing College, much bigger and far more imposing than anything the village had seen before. It consisted of three storeys, with four ornate pilasters dividing the house vertically into three regular sections, and it had two single-storied wings set at right angles to each end and running down towards the Everton Road, so that the house presented an inverted U-shape in plan. It looked out on a gravelled courtyard and a circular lawn. Behind the house were formal gardens, complete with statuary and a maze, and the small rectangular fishponds that so fascinated me when I was a boy. Beyond them was a large ornamental lake, behind which stood plantations of trees with walks laid out between them. In the distance on the horizon stood a red-brick folly, without which no eighteenth-century landscape was complete.

The park was described by Edmund Carter in his *History* of Cambridgeshire, published in 1753. Carter said that it was 'the most

Sir George Downing's house. Much of it is conjecture as the only surviving picture of the house is a tiny sketch made long after it was demolished.

agreeable and pleasant situation in all this country, having every beauty that nature can afford, nor hath art been wanting to complete it'. William Cole, less verbose, simply said that Downing had built 'a most elegant House'.

For the first time since the last of the Avenels, a person of some social standing and importance was living in the village. Just what this could mean to the other villagers one of them discovered the hard way: Edward Haylock was hauled before the Quarter Sessions in January 1713

for speaking [and] reflecting unmannerly words of her Majesties Justices of the peace for this County, and particularly of Sir George Downing, Baronet. And having upon his Appearance here this day in open Court *submissively begged pardon upon his knees* for his said offence, This Court doth therefore order that the said Edward Haylock be discharged.

The village, for so long free from the presence of a resident squire, had to swallow its pride and learn for a time anyway, that it was impossible for a man like Downing to exist without hordes of forelock-tugging people trailing in his wake. It would be unfair to lay too much blame on Downing. He was only asking for the same deference that every other man of wealth and position expected as a God-given right. 'God bless the squire and his relations, and keep us in our proper stations' was an attitude that most people, rich and poor, considered to be a fundamental fact of life.

I should think that those 'unmannerly words' of Haylock's were a joke he made about Downing's mansion (then being built) over a jug of ale in the Rose and Crown, and that he was overheard and reported by one of the constables, who all seem to have been inordinately fond of the place (the pub, not the mansion). It could be that Haylock made an injudicious comment about Downing's mistress. She was Mary Townsend, who began as a kitchen-maid in the East Hatley house. In 1722 she bore Sir George a daughter, christened Elizabeth.

In his later years, Downing passed his time quietly enough in the ample comfort of what was now known as 'Gamlingay Park'. He eventually reverted in old age to the family traits inherited through his father and grandfather, leading what Cole called 'a most miserable, covetous and sordid existence'. In 1744, while watching another of his follies (at Tadlow) being built, someone clouted Sir George on the head with a hammer and took several potshots at him. Coming on top of his gout this attack did his health no good at all and he died five years later, in 1749, lamented by very few.

Mary Townsend, perhaps piqued by the miserly £250 annuity she knew Downing had left her, took the opportunity to ransack the house and gathered all the money she could find. It amounted to £14,000 in sovereigns and several thousand pounds in banknotes. She had £4,000 buried in the garden and gave up the rest. It was not until after her death that the estate recovered the rest of the money. Her daughter received a £500 annuity as a legacy in her father's will.

Since Sir George left no heir his estates went to his cousin Jacob Garrard Downing, on condition that if Sir Jacob (as he now was) also died without leaving an heir the estates were to be used to buy some land in Cambridge on which to build a college.

Sir Jacob was described in fulsome terms by Edmund Carter in his *History* as 'a gentleman devoted to make the neighbourhood happy, having a very generous soul, and an extensive fortune,' – he could say that again – 'and so many amiable qualities that few inherit; and who is now very busy in improving the house and park, and employing many of the poor, who before wanted work'. I have no idea how he improved the park or employed the poor, but Sir Jacob Garrard Downing sounds far too good to be true. The reason for this exaggerated eulogy is that Downing was very much alive and kicking in 1753 when Carter was writing, and much too important to offend. However, Sir Jacob made sure that nobody inherited his amiable qualities by duly dying childless in 1763. Contrary to Sir George's will he left all his land to his wife. She in turn left it to her nephew, Captain Whittington. Then the complications began.

A protracted court case between the University of Cambridge and Sir Jacob's widow Lady Downing ended with judgement in favour of the University and should have led to the immediate founding of Downing's new college. Unfortunately for them, the redoubtable old widow and her friends had been canny enough to realise that possession is nine-tenths of the law and had grabbed the estate while they could. It took until 1800, and more litigation, before they were ousted, and until 1807 before the foundation stone of Downing College was eventually laid. Those years in London courtrooms had cost the College dear in more ways than one. Whether from perversity or a calculated piece of vandalism aimed at lessening the value of the property in Gamlingay when Lady Downing realised that she could never win, the fact is that the mansion, scarcely more than fifty years old, was torn down stone by stone until there was nothing left, and the materials sold for £800.

The remains are best seen from the air, where from 1,000 feet up the lake, hollows, terraces, circular lawn, plantations and the plan of the house are clearly visible to any passing aviator. On the ground it is still possible to look across the lake (drained in the nineteenth century but recently refilled), gaze at the trees Downing planted, the fishponds he once tended, and the crumbling remains of the folly, and ponder on the vagaries of men . . . and women.

25

The Poor

The most difficult thing about writing a book based largely on documentary evidence lies in knowing what to leave out. There are so *many* documents. Nowhere is this better illustrated than in the accounts of the overseers of the poor, who by the middle of the seventeenth century had become an entirely separate set of parish officers. Their accounts run only for a relatively short period of time – 1680 until 1734, with a few more from the end of the eighteenth and early nineteenth century – and even then they are by no means complete. Yet the copies I have number almost 700 separate sheets.

The award for the worst handwriting and the most eccentric spelling of any documents must go to the worthy compilers of these accounts, who expended so much energy in a losing battle with the English language. Unravelling the meaning is part of the fun of reading village documents.

The first half of the seventeenth century had seen the intractable problem of the poor growing ever more involved and time-consuming. Eventually two or more men found themselves working as unpaid overseers of the poor. They normally served six-monthly terms of office – quite long enough, they would probably have said – with monthly meetings known as 'town meetings' to discuss day-to-day business and any emergencies that the overseers felt unable to deal with on their own. These meetings, as most of the meetings seem to have been, were held in a village alehouse.

The main business of the overseers was, of course, providing for the poor and sick. The accounts usually have monthly lists of those receiving aid and the pitiful amounts they were given. Here, for the sake of comparison, are two such monthly lists, separated by a gap of fifty-one years. The amounts represent *weekly* payments only.

April 1682	s.	d.
William Ratford	1.	6.
Wido Brile	1.	6.
Bes Harper		8.
Wido Cooper	1.	0.
Marey Waren	1.	0.
Wido Lune		8.
Wido Evens		6.
Wido Gilbord	1.	0.
Nat Lune	2.	0.
John Farenton	1.	0.
Thomas Randol	1.	0.
Wido Tiler		6.
Widow Fisher	1.	0.
Ane Pane	2.	0.
John Pane	2.	0.
Edward Pane & James Pane	4.	0.
Widow Harker	2.	0.
Wido Besto		6.
	£1 3s. 10d.	

August 1733	s.	d.
Sarey Squire		6.
Will Rogers	1.	0.
Widdo Howard	1.	0.
Widdo Bigs	1.	0.
Widdo Peag	1.	0.
John Peack	1.	0.
Deab Streatt	2.	0.
John Meecks is deafghtor [daughter]	1.	0.
Widdo Morris		9.
Widdo Wooden	2.	0.

Widdo Mincks	1. 3.
Widdo Gray att Wellses	1. 3.
& for Salts child	1. 3.
Widdo Calburd	6.
Tho Watus [Waters] is child	1. 0.
Marey Willey	6.
Widdo Brown att Hincksworth	2. 0.
Humphrey Clare	3. 6.
Marey Cheavours	2. 0.
Recktor for Will Watus is child	1. 0.
Will Watus is child att Calburds	1. 0.
Tho Meecks is widdo	9.
Widdo Keeford	1. 6.
This account does not add	
upon the original document	£1 9s. 3d. (*sic*)

One notices straight away how little difference there is between the two accounts. The pittance paid for the relief of these old men, widows and children has hardly increased at all. How did they live on it? How *did* an old widow manage to survive on 1s. a week? I do not know. I should imagine they must have got some help from their friends and neighbours, otherwise they would not have lived for more than a week or two. Anne, John, Edward and James Paine were poor orphans in 1682 but they were quickly apprenticed and no longer a burden on the rates. The rest, though, remained 'on the parish' until death brought an end to their misery: and misery it was too. It could hardly have been anything else.

It is also noticeable that as time goes on the number of people who had to be supported by the parish went on growing. Support was not always freely given; 'I'm not paying to keep those idle so-and-sos' was as common an attitude then as it is today. The overseers were anxious to prevent any extra weight falling on the shoulders of the ratepayers, of whom the overseers themselves were often major contributors. In a rate made in 1629 'towards the reliefe of the poore' John Webb was rated at 4d. a month on his own account and 8d. a week for 'bringeing Robert Hallam, a poore man, into our parishe' without giving the required security. Gamlingay's poor rate was for the exclusive use of Gamlingay's poor, and woe betide anyone who ignored the fact. The parish records kept in the County Record Office in Cambridge are full of bonds taken out at the parish's instigation by employers and relatives of 'foreigners', intended to prevent any drain on parish funds. When a stranger tried to settle, or even dared to linger for a while, he or she was pretty soon moved on, forcibly if necessary.

1721

gave a woeman with child 2s. 2d., and to see hur out of ye town, 6d.

The danger of such a situation in the overseers' eyes was that if she had been allowed to stay, the woman might well have given birth in the village. This could have led to the child becoming chargeable to the parish, which would then be responsible for it – a situation to be avoided at all costs. If, as in this next entry, the woman was very close to actually giving birth it was imperative that the overseers acted swiftly.

1731

the day before Poton fare when the[y] brote the big beleyd woman with an order from Amtil [Ampthill, Bedfordshire].

Spent that nite at a towne meten	3. 0.
the next day mor[n]ing	1. 2.
And agreed with the man to marey the woman	1. 11. 6.
And paid for a lisance	1. 05. 0.
And paid pa[r]son for maring them	10. 0.
And ped for the clark	2. 6.
And for my time	1. 6.
	£3. 14. 8.

Although it was probably not amusing to the participants, this incident does have its funny side. It is rather like watching one of those speeded-up silent films: the overseers rushing all over the place like flustered hens, trying to decide what to do with a heavily-pregnant woman armed with an order giving her a claim on the parish; bribing 'the man' to marry her, dragging the parson off to church, and handing over a marriage licence with the ink still wet. The story is complete with a happy ending as the hastily-wed couple emerge from church to leave the village for ever, accompanied by the relieved smiles of the overseers as they mop their brows.

In cynical mood one is tempted to wonder whether it was all a trick. What could be easier than for a conveniently-padded woman to appear in a village and frighten the overseers into giving her money by pretending to be about to give birth to a child on the overseers' doorstep? And then to walk the mile or two into the next village and play the same trick there? Even better if a male accomplice could turn up, apparently willing to accept a pound or so for marrying a total stranger. The suspicion that the overseers, like the churchwardens, were sometimes gulled into parting with money seems to have occurred to this anonymous overseer in 1725, who gave

to a man & woeman & child *soposed* to have ye small pox to go out of Town, 7s. 6d.

Let's face it – it ought to have been plainly visible.

As for the indigenous poor, however, sometimes only a nudge was needed to remove from the village a man young enough and fit enough to seek his fortune elsewhere:

1720
gave John Street for to go Away, 5s.

Those who were too old or sick to leave the village relied on the overseers for their upkeep. We have just seen the small amounts of cash this involved. Beyond that, there was sometimes a little help with necessities like clothing, and food and fuel in times of dire need.

1718
boatt [bought] for Katt Dammak a pare of shues, 1s. 6d.
boatt for Katt Dammak a Goune; the Goune and making the Goune and threed Cost 7s. 6d.

That was in February. How had Kate Damack managed until then *without* a gown or a pair of shoes? Poor clothing, a bad diet, lack of warmth and general neglect meant that these people at the bottom of the heap were more likely to succumb to illness than the better-off villagers. It is no surprise to learn that when they were ill it was the overseers who had to pay for nursing them. Usually such care is dismissed in bald entries like 'Wodins Wife for A man and a Woman to Look atter, and for Vittels and Drinke, 2s.'. There are hundreds like that. But during a severe outbreak of smallpox, for example, the overseers were often stretched to the limit in trying to provide doctors, nurses and medicinal comfort. When John Kefford was desperately ill with the disease in 1731 the overseers were forced to act. This extract is rather long, but you would not get the complete picture if I shortened it much more.

The Charg about John Ceford, April 25 1731

	s. d.
Spent when wee met about smalpox	1. 2.
To pay to Master Peke for going to Cambrig	3. 6.
For myself and hos	3. 6.
For Mister Mede going back to Cambrig with os	1. 6.
For straw for the noses [nurses] to ley one	6.
For on lot of befe and seuit	1. 2.
To William Jaxon for nosen 9 days	9. 0.
Ped Widow Haris for shop-things an bred & boter	6. 11.
Ped Grigorey for waten on the smal pox	5. 6.
For seeing Ceferds deeds and spend	8.
For leing John Ceferd out	2. 0.
For bering John Ceferd in the nite	4. 6.
For his cofen, and bran and wole	8. 4.
Ped to the milir for a peke of whete	1. 1.
To Widow Ceferd before she le [lay] in, at 4 times	5. 0.
That nite as she ley in	2. 0.
To pay to the mid wife, nos Robeson	2. 6.
Ped to Omferey Thoroygood for 2 nites sleeping in her house	1. 0.
To Baker Web for 11 quarts strong, 12 smal [beer]	3. 3.

Bran was used for packing the corpse in the coffin. The wool purchased refers to an Act of Parliament passed in an attempt to aid the ailing wool-trade, which required every corpse to be buried in a woollen shroud and in a wool-lined coffin. Compliance was shown by production of an affidavit, and the buying of them features regularly in the accounts.

But what agonies of human suffering those clumsy words of the overseers must shelter! Anger at the social conditions that bred it and the indifference of the upper classes which fed it is pointless. One can only accept so much of this before one is forced to switch off one's emotions. Lengthy lists of funeral expenses, money for laying out the dead, endless and overwhelming evidence that despite doing their best the overseers were at the whim of nature soon leaves one unmoved, forced to adopt the attitude that the overseers themselves must have acquired before they had been in the job many weeks – the attitude which enabled a man to write dispassionately about 1s. spent 'for buring the dead man found in the feild'.

If the overseers, like doctors, could not allow themselves to become emotionally involved with the people they were trying to help, there must have been times when the job had its compensations. People *did* recover from sickness, orphaned children *did* grow up to reach adult-hood and lead a normal life, and widows sometimes survived quite well on their small allowances. When this happened the overseers deserved the pat on the back they probably gave themselves.

Cures continued to be performed by village healers armed with herbs, charms, closely-guarded remedies and a rudimentary know-ledge of anatomy. Sometimes they worked. In the 1720s the healer was Goody Eaton:

1720
Goodey Eatten for Curing Ladey Boner, and Curing Caulberd's Childs head and face, 3s. 6d.

1725
To Widdow Eaton for dressing Colburt Boy Legg, 3s.

1726
Paid to Goody Eaton for the Cure of John Grays Legs, 7s.

To my mind Goody Eaton's potions, ointments and bone-setting skills seem infinitely preferable – and certainly cheaper – than the bloodlet-ting antics of 'doctors'. And in case you are wondering who 'Ladey Boner' was – so am I. I cannot find a trace of her in any other record of the period. This tells me that she was one of the village poor, although she only appears a few times in the overseers' accounts and never in the lists of those getting relief. The only clue lies in an entry from 1722 when the overseers 'gave to My Ladey Boner towards a pare of shous, 1s.'. Ladey Boner *could* be a fallen aristocrat, but to me that entry sounds like heavy-handed sarcasm. Certainly the writer took great pleasure in recording it because it is written much bolder and larger than the rest.

The way the poor were treated reflects the harsh and often brutal methods that Acts of Parliament adopted to deal with them. None were designed to be more humiliating, or to put the poor more firmly in their place, than the Act passed at the end of the seventeenth century which forced each pauper, his wife and children to wear a badge on the right shoulder of their 'uppermost garment' showing a large letter 'P' (for pauper) and the initial letter of their parish. Unless the poor of Gamlingay were thus willing to be branded with the letters 'PG' they were deemed to be not entitled to their benefit, or were sent to the house of correction, whipped and put to hard labour for three weeks. Not surprisingly, there is some evidence that overseers up and down the country were reluctant to enforce this rule. These are the only entries I have discovered in the Gamlingay accounts:

1697
Paid for makeing the bages, 5s. 4d.

1703
Paid for cloath for Badges, 3s.
Paid for 18 badges making, 3s.
For threed to set on the badges, 2d.

1717
Payd Henrey Joans for 6 bages, 1s. 6d.

1719
Paid for 16 bages and setting on 4d.

1730
For 40 bags macking and cloth, $3\frac{1}{2}$d.

1735
For makeing 6 Bagges, 1s. 6d.

The very scarcity of these payments seems to indicate that either Gamlingay's overseers were slack in enforcing the law or so tight-fisted that they reused the badges when a pauper died.

When a pauper died the overseers had a claim on his personal belongings. He was only a pauper after all, and the parish had been put to a great deal of expense one way or another. Any money that could be raised was considered to be a partial repayment. It usually did not amount to very much. This is what the overseers made from selling Thomas Farington's goods in 1690:

	s. d.
For brakes	2. 0.
For his Coat & breches	3. 0
His Lether Coat & breches	3. 0.
For A blanket & a ketell	2. 0.
For his shoues and a blanket	1. 4.
For a Matock & bill & Cheares	4. 0.
For sithes, snathes & forke	3. 0.
For Chest	2. 0.
For A woole bedd	1. 0.
For A Table	1. 0.

That, I believe, is a typical inventory of a pauper's belongings. For Thomas Farington, lying on his simple bed and covered by a couple of blankets, death was perhaps a relief.

Thankfully, the overseers' accounts contain more than just death, disease, poverty and despair. They also contain their fair share of puzzles. I cannot for the life of me think why, in 1685/6, they made the following payments:

Item for wood & nalles & workman shep about the Crase tre, 1s.
Item payed to Frances Harvy for kepen of the felld for ten dayes at 8s.
Item payed for pouder & shot to the widdow Broun, 9½d.
Item given to the widdow Cuper for the Chindey man, 1s.

Presumably the 'Chindey man' was the village chimney-sweep, but why were the other payments made? The cross-tree which stood at the crossroads was obviously some sort of signpost, but this was normally the responsibility of the churchwardens. Try as I might I cannot see why the overseers were bothering with field-keeping. What did bird-scaring have to do with the poor – unless as a means of employment? Then again, why did they pay 5s. 'to A company of foot Souldiers on Candelmas fair day' in 1689? Perhaps because the soldiers threatened them if they did not pay up. The 'wheel' the overseers bought for Goody Rogers in 1703 is surely a spinning-wheel, with which she was no doubt expected to supplement the money they gave her – perhaps the same one mended ten years later when the overseers paid 'for a wheel & a reel broke by ye Mad woman'. But there is no ambiguity about 'digin a hol to emtey potes in'.

The overseers themselves came mostly from the class of people who left wills and inventories, and who to a large extent funded the poor rates. Sometimes the accounts reveal their differing attitudes towards their charges. One overseer will describe a man simply by his surname, to another he will be 'old so-and-so', and to some he will be 'poor so-and-so'. All of them, I think, must have cared about the plight of the poor or they would not have taken the job in the first place. Some perhaps cared more than others, human nature being what it is, but all in their turn tried to alleviate the worst effects of poverty. Now and again one finds evidence of the way they would dip into their own pockets when necessary. This is from 1721, when Stephen Apthorpe (one of the overseers) was repaid for expenses met from his own purse:

Alowed to Stephen Apthorp for money Lost bye his Rat [rate] that he never could gett, 1s. 6d.
Alowed him for A queire of paper, 1s.
Paid him for doctor Rolt, a bill for ye widow Wiges, 8s. 6d.

Incidentally, the Apthorpe habit of naming their sons Stephen appears to have confused them as much as it confused everyone else. Written at the end of the 1685/6 accounts are the words 'I am Stephen Apthorp': yes, but which one?

The overseers left themselves wide open to criticism when they paid out money to those whom the ratepayers felt did not need it, as this next item shows:

An upon the 17 of may i paid upon the town account on pound ten shillins and Eight pence to Wm Jeaps, *which was to the dis sattisfaction of some, but to my disadvantage*, and set it last in the Charges of may.

I wish I knew what that anonymous overseer was talking about. Why was paying the money to his disadvantage? Did his fellow villagers embarrass him with their comments? The affair must have preyed on his mind because he ended the accounts with these three quotations from the Bible:

I said in my hast all men are lyers.
I was naked and ye Clothed me not.
The poor you have with you allwais.

An apt note on which to leave the parish poor for the time being.

26

Loos Fellows and Rogs

The constable, like his counterparts the overseers and the church-wardens, had a difficult, thankless task. Occasionally it had a spice of danger too, as William and John Burley discovered. There had been a constable in the village since at least the early fourteenth century, but apart from one stray account from around 1629 the yearly accounts survive only from the period 1670 to 1740. Constables were appointed by the village, a tradition that continued until organised police forces were set up in the nineteenth century. Their primary duty was to keep the peace, but as with the other parish officers little odds and ends became (for no apparent reason) their particular responsibility. The constables' accounts are a mixture of items which should in theory have been the lot of somebody else.

Their chief responsibilities were the arrest of law-breakers, keeping a village watch, collecting certain taxes, removing vagrants, whipping recalcitrant beggars, supervising the alehouses and furnishing men for the militia. But open any of these accounts and what is the constable spending his time on? Relieving the poor, like everybody else. William Bestow's undated accounts of *c.*1629 begin with the heading 'Criples' and continue with sundry payments like 'given to pasengers that whent with pases', and 'for a Sick man that lay alnight', while in 1725 the constable was constantly being disturbed like this:

Paid to a dum Man att door, 2d.
Paid to a man att my door, 1d.
Paid to five saymen that came to my door, 1s.
Paid to Great Belley Woman, 2d.
Paid to Great Belled woman for to Gett hur out of the town, 2s. 6d.

Laying out a few pennies here and there to 'passengers' and moving them on to the next parish took up a great deal of their time. It was a task certainly not made any easier when the poor man or woman was mentally disturbed.

1678
Layd out to too men for holding A Crased woman in A Cart, 2s.; and to her 4d.
For A Scotchman which was distracted that John Wallis brought, his father not being at home, 3d.

Disbanded soldiers and sailors wandering around the countryside could likewise prove difficult:

Laid out to 2 disbanded souldiers that were disbanded at Diss in Norfolke, being Aged & Sick, 6d.
Layd out to 2 disbanded souldiers that came out of Flander sick, which had A Lawfull certificate signed by the next Justice A peace, 4d.

When the constable forked out 1s. in 1678 'to keep out the draggones' it had nothing to do with fabled beasts or his primitive imagination. They were, of course, dragoons.

Constables were used by the government as unpaid tax-collectors, riding hither and thither delivering money to this or that authority. John Webb in 1671 made quarterly journeys to Cambridge 'about the thre month tax', which was in fact the County rate. William Triploe paid 1s. 'for winder tax Bill' in 1725, an amount that might leave one wondering why the village possessed so little glass, were it not for an entry in a later set of accounts 'for windes sesements'. The shilling was to cover the cost of assessment, and not the actual amount of tax raised, which would not appear in the accounts in any case.

We came across the system of purveyance — buying goods for Royal use at reduced prices — as far back as the fourteenth century, and the practice continued. We of the twentieth century complain about being overtaxed, but how would we feel about being forced to contribute to a rate made by the constables for 'the provisioninge of fattlinge & powltrie for the Kinge Majesties howsold'? The taxpayers of Gamlingay had to do so in 1623, raising £4 1s. 8d. towards feeding James I. No wonder purveyance was so detested.

The constables had to keep the village bridges in good repair. There are many entries like 'paid to John Larkins for mend the Briges and the Rayles att puddle pitt'. As you might expect, they were also in charge of the village stocks:

For Mending the stocks: 2 shillings the smith had, and 6 pence the Carpenter had.

Peaid to Georg Langley for menden the stokes, 4d.

For mending the Iron work in the Stocks, 8d.

These were still in use from time to time, although this is the only instance recorded by the constables:

1725

Paid for Bear 1 shilling, when Henry Hart sat in the stocks.

Here is another instance of the ambiguity so often evident in these documents: was the beer for the constable or for Henry Hart? And what had Henry Hart done to be locked up in the stocks at the age of fifty-three? He was probably too old for it to have been anything as demanding as 'the man that Rid away with John Smiths horse' whom William Careless had to drag off to Cambridge Castle that same year.

It was to prevent such lawlessness that the constable was in charge of the village watch. This consisted of one or two men armed with a lantern and a staff, who walked round the village during the night on the lookout for evil-doers and calling out the time: 'ten o'clock and all's well'. Occasionally they apprehended a rogue:

Expences for Lodging A man taken up by the watch one night, 10d.

At other times they simply roused the slumbering constable for no good reason, as when Christopher Fickis was woken and hauled from his bed to visit 'the wach that night when Christopher Parsons suspechet Rogs', or when 'the wachmen as was . . . thought was some Loos fellows in the town'. 'Loos fellows' or 'Rogs', it was the constable's duty to check on it, and judging by the shilling or two spent on the watch each time I would guess that there was some sort of back-up system the constable could call on when necessary.

During daylight, catching a criminal was the responsibility of everyone in the parish. When a crime had been committed the victim was supposed to yell 'out! out! out!' at the top of his voice, warning the neighbours to arm themselves and join in the pursuit, sounding horns and shouting. All this din and commotion was supposed to alert the rest of the village. It was a very old idea, perhaps in use as far back as the seventh century, and definitely still in use 1,000 years later.

If the criminal managed to cross the parish boundary without being caught, the 'hue and cry' (as it was called) was passed on to the next village, and so on across the countryside, following the villain wherever he went. The accounts are full of examples. These are a few:

1670
For sendinge a Hew and cry to Everton, 4d.
Gave to John Buntinge for Carryinge off A hewandcry to Gransden, 4d.

1678
For Carrying a Hue & Cry to Potton, 2d.

1725
For my Going a bout town with Hu in Cry, 1s.

This method must have been fairly successful (or rather, nobody found anything better), but the records seldom tell much beyond the barest of bare facts, like this enigmatic entry from 1678:

For Carrying the Robbery money to the High Constable, 1s.

A dozen questions immediately spring to mind when reading that, but there are no answers. Neither will I ever discover why the constable paid 15s. 2¼d. 'for the Robery money' in 1735.

Moments of excitement were rare in the life of a humble village constable. Providing men and arms for the county militia was a more common event, but even here little information is forthcoming. This is from around 1629:

To the soldyers at Elsworth at the second trayneing their, 4s.

The militia was never universally popular. The Militia Act of 1757, intended to provide an army to repulse possible French invasion, sparked off some violent riots in Bedfordshire, particularly in the neighbourhood of Biggleswade. The fear was that some men might be forced to go overseas, and the primary concern of the rioters was to obtain and destroy the lists of men eligible for service being prepared by village constables up and down England. The Bedfordshire riots spilled over the county boundary into Gamlingay during the summer of 1757.

Lord Royston, son of Lord Hardwicke of Wimpole Hall, wrote to his father that there 'was a riot at Gamlingay last night, and the lists of that parish was taken by force from the chief constable. The man said it was dark, and he could not distinguish any of them but they threatened him hard if he did not deliver it up. The petty constables are afraid of doing their duty'. (This letter is quoted in *Law and Order in Georgian Bedfordshire*, by Eric Stockdale (Bedford, 1982).)

There was enough excitement there for anyone, I should think. I can add no more to this account because the constables' accounts for 1757 have not survived. Soon after these riots the government saw the folly of attempting to enforce such an unpopular law and dropped the idea.

Finally, before leaving the constables, there is one more item I must quote. This is from 1708:

Paid a man for going to Sr George Downings with a man that made a disturbance at Mr Freemans, 6d.

This was the Sir George Downing 'of unsound mind', father of the Sir George who built Gamlingay Park. Dotty or not, I have a shrewd idea that he knew exactly why the disturbance had taken place in that particular house, but we will have to take a step or two backwards in time in order to find out why.

27

Dissent

From the moment the Caxton Baptist church made its first convert in Gamlingay in 1652, nonconformity was to be an important part of village life. Its growth was due in part to the preponderance of farmers and tradesmen in the village, among whom nonconformism tended to flourish. A resident squire, through his economic and social control of people's lives, could stamp on dissent before it took root; the lack of such a resident squire in Gamlingay helped the fragile plant to grow. Just how rapid its growth was is shown by the Episcopal Returns of 1669, which record 'about 40' dissenters in the parish, described sourly as 'All (Except 5 or 6) of poore & very meane condition', and who were receiving instruction in a weekly conventicle. The following year the congregation in Gamlingay joined the Bedford General Meeting. This was run by the most celebrated of all seventeenth-century dissenters: John Bunyan, the author of *The Pilgrim's Progress* (1684). The minutes of the Bedford church record the facts:

The congregation also having taken into consideration the desire of Gamlingay friends to joyne with us, did agree that next meeting they should come over, and give in their experience.

The following week nine Gamlingay men were welcomed and received as members of the Bedford church. For the next forty years the Gamlingay Open Baptists belonged to the Bedford church.

Occasionally the Church held its meetings at Luke Astwood's house in Gamlingay, which was properly licensed for the purpose by the Quarter Sessions in Cambridge. These extracts from the church minute book give an idea of the strict upright religious bearing expected from the brethren:

At a Church meeting at Gamblingay the 18 of the 8th month was cast out of the Church the wife of our brother Witt, for railling and other wicked practises. Concluded that som dayes be sett appart for humiliation with fasting and prayer to God becaus of som disorders amongst som of the congregation, specialy for that som have run in to debt more than they can satisfie, to the great dishoner of God and scandall of religion.

At a Church meeting holden at Gamblingay . . . our sister Landey withdrawn from, the causes were for that she had withdrawn communion from the saints, had despised gifts in the Church, had taught her children to play at cards, and remained impenitent after severall admonitions.

Complaint was made against brother William Robinson of Gamlingay, that he was going to marry a carnall maid, and would not be perswaded to the contrary. Twas therefore concluded that he should be publickly admonished at Gamlingay before the Lord's Supper etc.

The emphasis on good business practice – the statement that getting into debt was 'to the great dishoner of God and scandall of region' – is indicative of the background of many church members. They could not afford to be anything but strict. After 1660 the various Puritan sects which had sprung up in England during the Commonwealth were subjected to a lot of pressure from the authorities. Despite this persecution (or perhaps because of it) the sects grew in numbers and strength. To them it was simple: the Anglican Church was propounding erroneous doctrine and they would continue to defy it. Many harmless dissenters suffered greatly: Bunyan himself was imprisoned from 1660 until 1672, albeit rather loosely at times, and none could really feel safe until the Toleration Act of 1689 put an end to persecution.

Bunyan preached in Gamlingay on many occasions. There is even a story about him giving a lift on his horse to a Sister Beaumont from her home in Edworth to the meeting in Gamlingay. It was doubtless his example and passionate conviction which helped sustain the faith of the Gamlingay members during the difficult times before the Toleration Act was passed.

In the long run there was not much the Church of England could do about the dissenters. According to the Compton census of 1676 there were forty-four of them in the village (plus one papist), and twenty-four people were presented at the archdeacon's visitation in 1682 for failing to attend the parish church. The ecclesiastical courts, like their manorial counterparts, had lost their power, and nobody took them very seriously any longer.

Even those members of the Anglican Church who remained loyal to the Church of England were sometimes not impressed with the quality of the clergy engaged in doctrinal battle with the nonconformists. Elie Barnes was presented in 1686 for quarrelling with, striking and doing violence to the curate, Robert Humphrey, and for breaking his leg '*and afterwards wishing it had been his neck*'! That same year *150* people were presented for not attending divine service. I do not suppose that all of them were dissenters, but the figure shows the indifference generated among ordinary folk by the Church of England.

By 1710 the long tramp on horseback to attend church meetings in Bedford was proving too much for the brethren in Gamlingay. All thirty of them asked to be collectively released ('by reason of their distance from us') so that they could build their own chapel in the village, parts of which still survive in the present Baptist chapel.

This brings us back to Mr Freeman, and the man who made a disturbance at his house in 1708. Richard Freeman, 'a Protestant Dissenter' whose house was 'lycenced for the Worshipp of God' by the Quarter Sessions, had settled in Gamlingay as the Baptist preacher in 1699. The disturbance was probably caused by someone who hotly disagreed with his independent views and got himself arrested for his trouble.

Freeman and the Baptists thrived despite the opposition; Freeman in fact once preached to an enormous congregation of 250 people. Dissent was all the rage. Bartholomew Webb, a Quaker, had his 'Dwelling house and Malthouse' licensed as a meeting-place. The Anabaptists gained a footing too. The Church of England was helpless in the face of such enthusiasm, hanging on as best it could while its clergy grew increasingly further apart from its falling congregation.

Nonconformity became an established part of village life, but the nonconformists could not relax their vigilance. Church members were expected to lead blameless lives and, being human, many of course failed. Many of the people we have met in this book only appear because for one reason or another they failed to live up to the expectations of authority. These brief extracts from the Gamlingay Baptist church minute books illustrate similar weaknesses. I have also included one or two other noteworthy items:

1712
Sister Martin found guilty of 'unlawful Love unto Thomas Meeks . . . and for the same she was Authoritively Admonished in the presence of the church'.

Sister Damack guilty of 'presumptuous Lying and in puting Brother Freeman upon Reproveing of sister Ann Jeaking for her pride'.

1717
Day of prayer 'to Humble our selves Before God, and to Intreat his favor and mercy unto us on Behalf of the prevailing distemper, the smal pox . . . and Remove it from the Town, and especially from his own people'.

1722
Rose Robinson guilty of 'Being disordered with drink at goodman Chesham's on the night on which the shoe-makers keep a feast, and did very often urge and presse on other carnal people to sing vain and heathenish Love Songs . . .' Admonished and suspended.

Thomas Meeks found guilty of fornication. Excommunicated.

Complaint about 'people Bringing Doggs' to Church. Thomas Moss paid 6s. to 'Beat them away' and to 'Looke after the children that are Rude or play at the meeting or in the meeting-yard'.

1725
Day of prayer and fasting 'to Stop the Bottles of heaven, and Restraine the great Rains . . . that the hay Might be gathered in without further damage, and the grain harvist might be Ripened . . .'

Brother Careless confessed to 'Being at the Ale house the Satterday night Before the church meeting with his wife, with some other carnal men and staid all the night until the Lord day morning did appear'. Admonished.

1729
Jonathan Philip accused of 'excess of drinking and tippling at Ale-houses'. Admitted he 'had sometimes drunk too much'.

1732
John Underwood guilty of 'stealing his Master's grain and deceiving his wife in marriage about his debts . . .'. Admonished.

1742
Brother and Sister Bowd excommunicated because it was 'plainly Manifest that they were both Guilty of fornication'.

1770
Edward Billing, the pastor, guilty of 'Exesive Drinking' and 'Neglecting the Dutys of his Family'. Discharged as minister and pastor.

1772
Mary Garret 'publickly caught in the act of fornication'. Excommunicated.

1795
Epidemic of smallpox. It was 'thought proper to inoculate the inhabitants in general who had not had it . . .'.

28

The Gulf Widens

Given the growth of nonconformism in the village, one might have expected the Anglican Church to have made some effort to reclaim at least some of its lost congregation. Instead, it slumbered. For much of the eighteenth century the vicar was an absentee, usually employing a curate to hold services for those who felt the need to attend. The rectorship had for a long time been a mere sinecure, whose incumbents collected their tithes but otherwise ignored the parish. On the other hand, the dissenters were village people, and this gave them an advantage. Setting aside religious doctrine, it must have seemed to the ordinary villager that the Church of England had forgotten them and was simply using the income from the parish to subsidise the gentrified lifestyle of its distant clergy. It is not surprising that dissent flourished.

But the dissenters did not have things all their own way. The scales had already tipped back a little in favour of the established Church when in 1802 Robert Hepworth was ordained as vicar. He at least was resident in the vicarage. He took his own services, too, although he complained that most families in the parish were dissenters, and that only twelve or thirteen people received the sacrament. The vicar who succeeded him, Mr J B James, took the fight to the nonconformists.

The battlefield was education. The village had never been very enthusiastic about this issue. True, there was a small school attached to the meeting-house and there had been a succession of day-schools for those who could afford the fees. But while by the early nineteenth century most other villages in the county were sending roughly one in eleven of their children to school, Gamlingay could only manage the abysmal ratio of one in 225. Both Dissenters and Anglicans ran Sunday schools, but the crying need was obviously for some kind of day-school offering cheap education to the children of the village.

What Gamlingay actually got only serves to show to what ridiculous lengths the opposing churches were prepared to go in order to outdo one another. They *both* built schools. In 1848 a National School and school-house were built by the Church of England to accommodate 160 pupils. The *Cambridge Chronicle* reported that when it was opened the children were given a dinner (after a sermon) of roast beef and plum-pudding, which was probably the first time most of them had tasted such culinary delights. Not wishing to waste such a golden opportunity to beat the drum for the Church the children were walked in procession round the village, and after more organised merrymaking the children were sent home with the words of the national anthem ringing in their ears. Education usually meant indoctrination first, instruction second.

Anglican pride was dented when, in the very same year, the Baptists opened their own school next door to the chapel. The opening festivities probably matched those of the national school – I cannot report them because the *Chronicle* failed to send a correspondent along – but it would not surprise me if the very same children who had enjoyed the vicar's treat also consumed the food supplied by the Baptists.

There was no doubt that two schools was one too many. It soon became clear that the one to suffer was the Church of England national school, as anyone might have foreseen. It could only muster about half the attendance of its rival, the Baptist's British school, and by 1861, although it was only thirteen years old, it was described as a 'dilapidated old place', and closed shortly afterwards.

Apart from building twice the required number of schools, the rivalry between the two factions expressed itself in a rash of other buildings designed to express the good taste and status of their respective members. The Baptists rebuilt the original meeting-house in 1840 in solid, respectable style. A new rectory was also built at about the same time (the distinction between rector and vicar was abolished and the two united in one rectorship in the middle of the nineteenth century). The Methodists built a chapel of their own when they arrived in 1833, and the Primitive Methodists erected a chapel in Green End in 1855. The Particular Baptists had their own chapel from the early years of the century, but, not wishing to be outdone by the other sects, built the Zoar chapel in 1866 as their contribution to a village by now overflowing with four chapels, a church, two schools and an apparent excess of zeal.

The village was gradually leaving behind the old-established, slow-changing ways it had followed for hundreds of years in other ways, too. The roads were still a problem, but two of the most heavily used were turnpiked. The first was the Waresley to Potton road, incorporated as part of the Bury and Stratton Turnpike in 1755. In 1814 the road to St Neots became part of the St Neots and Potton Turnpike. Road-users had to pay a toll, the money being spent on repairs. The rest of the parish roads were as ill-managed as they had always been.

The village inns had all acquired names by the eighteenth century, and these now assume a more familiar ring. It is difficult to say exactly how many inns there were in the village. The numbers fluctuated slightly over the years, but the thirsty villagers sustained nine inn-holders in 1735, and some ten or eleven occur regularly in the licensed victualler's registers thereafter (the registers are kept in Cambridge County Record Office). Some inns, like the Cock and the Falcon, were old-established ones. Others, although later establishments, con-tributed some fanciful names to the village scene. There was the Blue Ball, the Castle, the Dolphin and the Chequers, as well as the Wheat-sheaf and the Plough; the village also boasted the Thatch't House, the Wheel, Three Horse Shoes and the Swan and Grapes.

Other new buildings sprang up all over the village, especially in Mill Street, following another fire. It happened in 1812, and the Cambridge Chronicle was at the scene. The fire began, the paper said, about ten o'clock in the morning in Thomas Wright's wheelwright's yard, the fire from the forge setting a thatched roof nearby alight. Mr Woodham's barns and outbuildings were destroyed, then the fire:

continued its dreadful ravages along both sides of Mill-street, burning down 22 dwelling-houses, six barns, and a great many outbuildings, when the arrival of an engine from Potton prevented the further extension of the flames, but which continued burning furiously amidst the ruins till nine o'clock in the evening . . . The calamity, however, falls heavy upon the occupiers of the houses destroyed, 18 of whom are deprived of their homes.

The paper announced in its next issue that it took much pleasure in stating that a subscription had been started for 'the sufferers by the late fire in Gamlingay'. When it was known that eighteen poor families had been 'reduced to the utmost distress' by the blaze, the paper felt sure that 'the benevolence of the public will not be solicited in vain'.

Apart from the arrival of the horse-drawn fire-engine which rattled over from Potton, there is really very little difference between this fire and the one reported to the Privy Council 200 years earlier. Even the appeal for funds is the same. How helpless the village still was in the face of natural disaster – and how often history repeats itself.

Agriculture had not changed much. It was still carried on in the great open fields as it always had been, although more and more people were becoming convinced that the land would have to be enclosed before any real progress could be achieved. In 1794, Vancouver's *General View of the Agriculture in the County of Cambridge* described the loamy sand soil to the east of the village as being 'proper for the culture of barley, turnips, rye, and clover'. The 'thin, cold, hungry clay, lying upon a gault' was good – if that is the right word – for producing wheat, beans, peas, clover and black oats. The meadows were of a 'moory nature', while there were about 'twelve hundred of the common Cambridgeshire sheep' kept in the parish, 340 of which 'perished in the course of last year, by the rot, and the mortality at this time still continues'. Gamlingay's farmers said that it was due to the 'bad state of the drainage, in the open fields'. Without enclosure and proper drainage 'no improvement can possibly be made in the stock and husbandry of this parish'.

It was to be another fifty years before the enclosure of the open fields, which Vancouver clearly thought vital to the village, was to come about.

Talking of the century between 1750 and 1850 will probably bring to mind the industrial revolution, the coming of the railways, development of commerce – in fact, 'progress'. But there was little of it here. For the rural villages of much of southern England it was a period of stagnation, decline, repression and despair.

One can describe the history of England from the Middle Ages onwards in terms of the relative gap between rich and poor becoming slowly wider over the centuries. Looked at in that way, this century sees the gap rapidly increasing until it becomes a vast chasm, with the broad mass of labourers and paupers on one side, and the self-confident land-owning squirearchy and farmers on the other.

In 1279 the gap was small, and mainly economic. There was not a lot of difference in attitude between the free peasant holding twenty or thirty acres, and the bondsman with an acre or two and his cow, holding his land in return for working for his lord. Both lived in similar houses, both worked the land themselves with the aid of their families, and both were dependent on each other's co-operation in order to make a living. They knew each other well, often worked side by side in the open fields, and they understood each other. The chances are that they were also related. It was not a perfect world by any means, as we have seen.

By the early nineteenth century the gap between the pauper living in his tumbledown cottage with a few sticks of furniture to his name and the farmer in his large, comfortable farmhouse was enormous. The farmer, living off the profits from hundreds of acres of land tilled by a small army of labourers, was a world apart in values, attitudes and understanding from his men. Farmers tended to look down on their men as little better than beasts. The rift between them meant that neither men nor masters could see the others' point of view. The patriarchal, pipe-smoking, church-going farmer and the sullen, resentful, ill-educated, poorly-fed and poorly-clothed labourers feared and despised each other. And there was little chance that they would be related.

As an example of economic difference I want to take a look at two documents. Joseph Triplow died a pauper in 1804. These are his worldly possessions as seized by the overseers:

Deal Table
Dresser & shelves
5 Chairs
Grate
Pothooks, Tongs etc
Tureen
Cupboard
Brown Table
Tea Kettle
Milk Kettle
Warming Pan
Bed & one Blanket
Bedstead & Curtains
4 Chairs 2 Boxes
One Window Curtain

I think we can safely assume that Joseph Triplow never tasted roast beef. He probably never tasted meat unless he managed to poach an occasional rabbit or hare. Instead, he existed on a diet of potatoes, bread and weak tea, perhaps (as many people did) resorting to soaking a piece of toast in hot water to give an impression of tea when times were really bad.

At the other extreme, let us look at how William Careless lived. He farmed the Merton estate and lived in the manor farmhouse. The College surveyed the estate in the early nineteenth century and found:

a large Farm House built of Timber & Lath & Plaister . . . in very good repair: a Brewhouse in tolerable repair – Dovehouse in very good condition, a Cart Hovel newly-built & boarded on the backside. Stables of Timber, boarded & thatched, in good condition; a Granary part brick, part boarded & thatched, in good repair. A wheat Barn & Rye Barn (lately new boarded & thatched by the Lessee). A Barley Barn of Timber boarded & thatched in good repair, & a Chaff House boarded & thatched, in want of Repair. In addition to these buildings – a Wheat Hovel, Wheat House, Cow House & Hen House, a Wood Barn in the orchard & Hogstye in the Farm yard are claimed by the Lessee as his own Property.

William Careless's horses were better housed (and better fed) than the likes of Joseph Triplow.

So much for the economic difference. Things were made infinitely worse by the fact that power was concentrated in the hands of the land-owners and farmers. Land-owners controlled Parliament, which passed savage laws protecting property. Their tenants – substantial farmers like William Careless – controlled the labourers through their monopoly of employment, and the fact that it was they who provided the bulk of the money for the poor rates. And it was generally the farmers, or people of their class and sympathy, who served as overseers and dished out the money they themselves had contributed in the first place.

The Poor Laws started as a reasonably workable solution to the problem of poor people unable to maintain themselves. By the 1790s they had become a prison for the rising number of labourers. The parish boundaries were their prison walls, outside which they were barely-tolerated intruders. Inside them they could at least claim some sort of relief, however miserable.

Those who tried to escape by running away suffered severe punishment if they were caught. William Birx tried it, failed, and found himself standing before the Cambridge Quarter Sessions in 1791, 'committed by Edward Leeds, Esquire, for running away and leaving his Family chargeable to the Parish of Gamlingay'. He was found guilty, needless to say, and ordered to be

publickly whipped to morrow at Cambridge, confined to hard Labour one Month in the House of Correction, then publickly whipped at Cambridge and discharged.

Presumably he would be sent back to Gamlingay and the family he deserted. Birx was probably encouraged in his attempt to run away by the success of James Wash four years earlier. Wash was never caught, despite the reward of one guinea advertised in the *Cambridge Chronicle* for information leading to his recapture, and this picturesque description of the twenty-six year old Wash as: 'of middle size, wears his own black hair, his upper lip very thick, round shouldered and knap-knee'd'. What a short distance the poor men of England had travelled since the Middle Ages: from bondsmen to landless paupers.

The number of poor labourers was growing all the time as men who had managed to eke a living from a couple of acres of land gave up the unequal struggle and became full-time wage-earners. Their position worsened after the adoption in 1795 of the so-called Speenhamland System of relief. This was in effect a scale by which the pauper and his family received a certain sum each week, related to the cost of a loaf, in addition to wages. It did not take the larger farmers very long to grasp the fact that they no longer had to pay a man a living wage, because the difference between what they paid and what was needed to live on would be made up out of the poor rates. It meant that large farmers, with big labour forces, benefited at the expense (literally) of the small independent farmer who employed little or no labour. The contributions of the small farmer to the poor rate helped subsidise the labourers on the bigger farms. Thus even a labourer in full-time employment became a pauper without rights through the adoption of Speenhamland, and many small farmers were forced off the land.

The result of introducing the Speenhamland System into Gamlingay was that eight of the largest farmers got together and agreed a very low, *maximum* wage among themselves. Obviously it was no good one farmer paying more than another. How do I know this? Because they were so sure of themselves that they even had the temerity to note their agreement in the pages of the overseer's accounts. Here it is:

We whos names are herinunder written have determined and agreed to give the Labours not exceeding seven shilling Per week.

Wm Woodham	Joseph Ingle
James Paine	Tho Trustram
John Edwards	Wm Mead
John Francis Guy	Wm Careless

Date Nov 6 1797

The labourers' position remained insecure and miserable throughout the early years of the century, until the end of the Napoleonic Wars in 1815 signalled the end of the wartime price boom. Even the larger farmers began to feel the pinch. The labourers were harder pressed than ever, and discontent rumbled dangerously throughout the country during the next fifteen years, breaking out in such sporadic and uncoordinated disturbances as the Littleport Riots, the burning of ricks and machine-breaking. It culminated in 1830 in the last great rural revolt, a disorganised, emotive expression of despair known as the 'Swing Riots'. They got their name from the anonymous letters which were sent to particularly hated farmers, threatening them with arson – and worse – if they refused to meet the labourers' demands; the letters were signed by the mythical 'Captain Swing'.

There were outbreaks of machine-breaking (threshing machines in particular) in many of Gamlingay's neighbouring villages towards the end of 1830, especially in Huntingdonshire. Oddly enough, although Gamlingay was one of the worst unemployment blackspots in Cambridgeshire, there is no evidence of any demonstrations against the farmers in the village. The atmosphere was highly charged, nonetheless, and the authorities were ready to crack down on anyone they suspected, however remotely, of involvement in the disturbances. Thus it was that the *Cambridge Chronicle*, firmly on the side of authority, reported sadly in its issue of 31 December 1830 that:

During the past week strict investigations have been made into the case of Joseph Saville, committed to Bury gaol on the charge of dropping inflammatory letters signed 'Swing' – and several communications have passed between the magistrates and the Secretary of State, by whom a search of the prisoner's house at Gamlingay, in this county, was ordered last Saturday, and the governor of Bury gaol proceeded thither for the purpose. But although it appears Saville has practised the dropping of letters to a great extent, and a letter has been found, which alludes in a mysterious manner to one of the fires in Huntingdonshire, (where he was at the time when it occurred) *the expectation of bringing home to him any charge of participation in these acts has not been realised.*

(My italics.) The 'last Saturday' given as the day Saville's house was searched was Christmas Day 1830 – a nice present for his wife Mary and their six children, already robbed of the breadwinner. Saville was one of the small farmers impoverished by the agricultural depression after 1815. Hence his literacy and hence his probable bitterness. Interestingly enough, his father-in-law was Thomas Trustram, one of the eight farmers who signed the maximum wage agreement in 1797 (the year Saville married his daughter), which was the turning-point in the decline of the smaller farmer in Gamlingay. The *Chronicle* had clearly found Saville guilty; had a court done so, he could have been executed.

The revolt failed, ending in defeat for the labourers and provoking an almost unbelievably vicious backlash from the landed classes, who (quite rightly) saw themselves threatened by the rebellious lower orders. Some changes were effected, mainly in the operation of the Poor Law, which was drastically overhauled for the first time in 200 years. Poor Law commissioners were despatched all over the country with instructions to report on its operation.

29

Alfred Power and the Stone Pickers

Alfred Power, esquire, was given the task of looking at the way the Poor Law functioned in Cambridgeshire. His report was published in 1833 in a volume called *Extract of reports to the Poor Law Commission*. Power said that the poor rates in Cambridgeshire were used in three main ways. First of all, there was 'the permanent weekly pay' given to the old, the impotent poor and to widows. Then there were the wages paid to paupers working for the parish. Finally there was the money paid to the 'occasional and casual' poor – those suffering 'real or pretended' sickness and the men whose earnings were made up to a subsistence level by the overseers. But it was when he wanted an example of the appalling mess parishes could get into by applying a system of relief unsuitable for the problems caused by large numbers of paupers, that Alfred Power turned his attention to Gamlingay.

There were, he said, 'few worse examples of oppressive rates, aggravated by extreme mismanagement, than the parish of Gamlingay'. He went on:

The present population is 1319. The advantages afforded by the waste land in a supply of fuel, and the permission to build cottages on it, have attracted the poor from the neighbouring parishes; and a vast quantity of settlements have been made by the farmers letting their land during a part of the year to be dug for potatoes at high rents. As many as thirty families have been introduced in this way.

In other words, farmers were providing 'foreigners' with a legal settlement in order to get the high rents. Most of these outsiders settled on the inhospitable and isolated Heath. The extra burden on the rates was met by all the ratepayers, and not just farmers. The consequence was, of course, that the rates went on rising year by year.

The eldest of my informers (all occupiers) remembers the poor-rate amounting to only £50 – that was sixty years ago [i.e., in the 1770s]; the expenditure of the year ending March, 1832, was £1427.

That is roughly a twenty-eight-fold increase in just sixty years. But in terms of the annual rateable value of the parish there had been an even bigger increase, because the annual rateable value was assessed at £2,945 in 1815, yet at only a little more than £2,000 in 1832.

The rates, therefore, have already approached to very nearly 15s. in the pound, and the constant decrease of capital and cultivation threatens a further augmentation. The increase of the last over the preceding year was £100. The disbursements of the last year stand thus:

Aged, impotent and widows	£318
Paupers working for parish	615
Materials, tools, & c.	54
Occasional casual poor relieved for sickness, & c.	316
Medical attendance	54
Law expenses, removals, & c.	17
Bastardies	10

Although this ancient, shambling, rambling system was patently on its last legs, it was only when Power examined those wages paid to paupers working for the parish that he discovered the really ludicrous side of the picture. He tells us that single men earned about 6s. from their employers, and married men from 9 to 10s. a week. The 'magistrates' scale' in use added the following amounts to their wages out of the poor rate:

A single man	3s.
Man and wife	5s.
Ditto with one child	6s.
Ditto with two children	7s.
Ditto with three children	8s.
Ditto with four children	9s.

Power went on to say that there were now between seventy and eighty men and boys employed by the parish, with an average throughout the year of about forty. He continued:

The sole employment is that of *collecting stones from the surface of the land*, for which they are paid at the rate of 2d. per bushel, until they have earned the sum allowed by the bread scale, *they then do as they please for that week*.

This account 'seemed rather a puzzling one'. Power could not understand why the paupers continued to be employed as stone-pickers. Surely they would have run out of stones sooner or later? Neither could he understand how, with stones fetching 1½d. a bushel, only about £11's worth or so were sold, to be set against the £615 it cost to pay the paupers. Power admitted that he was 'not fully satisfied'.

I am not surprised. It certainly does not make sense. But there was a simple explanation, so obvious that I wonder that the astute Mr Power did not realise what it was until later, when he was

leaving the village, after finishing my inquiries I encountered a group of boys and men, eight or ten in number, from the age of sixteen to twenty-five, about a stone heap, busily employed, some with their hands, some with large sticks by way of bats, *in returning the collected stones to the impoverished acres*.

Brilliant! That answered Power's doubts about the employment running out, and also explains why only £11 10s. appeared on the balance sheet for stones sold; and finally, it explains why the parish paid out £615 on 'paupers working for parish'. As a costly but effective way of providing unending employment, as a way of ensuring the labourers lost all sense of dignity and pride in their work, and as an almost total waste of everybody's time, it was an unbeatable system. Someone, surely, must have realised the

utter futility of paying one lot of paupers to pick up the stones, and another lot to put them all back again?

Power's report continued:

My interview with the overseers (the appointment I had made with them having become known) was voluntarily attended by about six of the other principal occupiers. The external appearance of these men betokened a want of agricultural capital; and they spoke of their parochial burthens in a despairing and almost reckless tone. They could not help themselves. They had in vain attempted several times to share the whole labour of the parish amongst themselves, according to the extent of each man's occupation . . .

Apparently, a strong practical objection to this scheme was that pay night occurred weekly, whereas the rate collector only called fourteen times a year. They had tried to employ the poor in draining the unenclosed fields, but the protests of the ratepayers who owned or rented land already enclosed, and who did not feel inclined to pay towards improving unenclosed land, killed off the idea. Under these circumstances 'they seemed to have abandoned all thought of mitigating their burthens by a strict and proper administration of parochial affairs'.

So far had they lost sight of 'public principle' that at the same time as forking out £615 a year without return, the parish officers were defending an indictment at the Quarter Sessions for the 'infamous' state of the parish roads. 'On this point', said Alfred Power, 'I am bound to say that, if the evidence be properly arranged, they must suffer a verdict.' It was, and they did. The parish was fined £150, which it was ordered to bestow upon repairing the roads.

This disgraceful state of affairs, and the misery it brought to the labourers in particular, was summed up by Alfred Power in a judgement which it is very difficult to disagree with. Gamlingay consisted of 'an impoverished race of farmers' who were 'screwing down a miserable, ill-lodged, and ill-fed population to the very letter of the bread-scale, and with difficulty producing their rates . . .'.

It was the farmers who had grabbed the chance to cut wages in the 1790s, the farmers who introduced the bread scale, the farmers who allowed so many newcomers to settle in the village for the sake of a quick profit, and the farmers who failed to put aside some capital during the boom years of the Napoleonic Wars. It was the farmers who pauperised the labourers, and the farmers' own selfish greed that was mainly responsible for the appallingly stupid application of the Poor Laws. In the end it was the farmers who suffered – but the labourers and their families suffered vastly more. And it was Parliament who finally put an end to this sorry state of affairs.

In response to the overwhelming evidence of mismanagement on a national scale that reached the Commission, the government took away the independence of parishes and ordered the formation of local Poor Law unions. It was not a perfect solution, but at least it removed some of the worst excesses of the old system. From 1835 Gamlingay became part of the Caxton and Arrington Union. After a year in operation the chairman, the Earl of Hardwicke, reported a saving in expenditure of about £2,600 in the first year, although

. . . it is to be remembered that this reduction has taken place without the aid of a workhouse. We put up a hand corn-mill during last winter, which employed 17 or 18 able-bodied men for a short time, but it was difficult to find hands to keep it at work.

With regard to the condition of the labouring classes, I should say that *a visible alteration has taken place in their manners;* all farmers I have conversed with, say that they are *more respectful and civil in their behaviour*, and more regular to their time of work. The parishes in the Union have never been so free from crime.

In Gamlingay 'the saving has been enormous' and the able-bodied have been employed during the winter, generally never having more than about '17 to 20 out of work at any one time', which compared very favourably to previous winters when a hundred men on average were receiving relief.

The New Poor Law of 1834 was much stricter than the old one. Outdoor relief was abolished and all recipients of relief were made to enter the workhouse (one was soon built for the Caxton and Arrington Union). The workhouse was deliberately made to resemble a prison. Families were broken up, the diet was poor, all 'luxuries' of life were excluded and special workhouse dress had to be worn. In rural areas, however, two good harvests following the introduction of the New Poor Law and the demand for labour to build the railways, together with the removal of the excesses and abuses of the allowance system largely eradicated the problem of rural pauperism – but not rural poverty. The workhouse was to remain a spectre which haunted the labourers and their families for another hundred years.

30

Transportation

If the treatment the common people received at the hands of their employers seems bad, then the punishments meted out to those who dared to infringe the property rights of the landed gentry were far worse. Barbarous sentences for petty offences were the rule. When I read such cases as the Gamlingay examples from the Quarter Sessions below, I often find myself unable to believe that Englishmen could treat their less-well-off fellow countrymen in such inhuman ways, apparently without the slightest feelings of injustice, or any sense that they were overreacting. In many ways the Quarter Sessions had taken over the role of the manor court, as you will see from these examples. Remember the average weekly wage of a labourer as you read the fines imposed.

1815
John Skinner, labourer, given three months in the house of correction, the last month of which to be in solitary, for assaulting the constable.

1822
William Ibbett, labourer, fined £10 with costs for cutting some branches off a walnut tree.

1830
John Boon fined £1 and 2s. damages and 3s. costs for stealing two hurdles.

1831

James Sell, labourer, given two months in the house of correction with hard labour for poaching.

Thomas Kefford and David Whitbread, labourers, fined 5s. with 5s. damages and 19s. 6d. costs for having 'cut, broken and thrown down . . . part of a certain hedge'.

1833

William Crissal, alias Harris, labourer, 'maliciously damaged a hedge' and was fined 10s., ordered to pay 6d. damages and 11s. costs.

1834

John Paine fined £5 with £1 16s. 7d. costs for poaching.

It is difficult to believe that the punishment fitted the crime when reading those extracts (there are many more I could quote). William Ibbett, for instance, fined £10 in 1822 for cutting some branches off a walnut tree, was a twenty-seven year old unmarried labourer. His earnings would have been 8 or 9s. a week at the time. How was he to pay his fine? The £10 fine represented almost half a year's income. Imagine being fined half *your* yearly income for an offence as trivial as that.

The fact that a prisoner, usually a labourer, could be convicted on little more than the word of a 'gentleman' who believed him to be guilty, led in extreme cases to blatant miscarriages of what was rarely 'justice' in the first place:

1821

Hall Parcel, aged 27, shoemaker, 'an Evil disposed person' charged with having obtained 30 bushels of potatoes worth 20s. under false pretences, and having stolen five sheepskins worth 12s. *Verdict*: guilty. *Sentence*: to 'be transported for the term of 7 years to such place beyond the Seas as his Majesty shall by and with the advice of His Most Honorable Privy Council think fit . . .'

1827

Stock Criswell, alias Harris, aged 23, labourer. Found guilty of stealing 'a bed quilt, pillow-case, a pair of black stockings, a round towel, a single stocking, and about half a pound of cheese'. *Sentence*: transported for 7 years.

1835

Samuel Gilbert, aged 21, labourer, and John Baines, aged 23, labourer. Found guilty of stealing 'one live tame duck' worth 1s. *Sentence*: both men transported for 7 years.

1844

Lewis Flint, aged 26, labourer. Guilty of stealing a pocket-knife worth 1s., and 1s. 11d. cash. *Sentence*: transported for 10 years.

1847

Elizabeth Bartle, spinster, servant. Guilty of stealing a sovereign (a coin worth 20s.) and a broach worth 5s. from her employer. *Sentence*: transported for 7 years.

1851

John Gilbert, aged 26. Guilty of stealing 20 stone of flour. *Sentence*: transported for 7 years.

1851

Edmund Yourby. Guilty of stealing £1 7s. 6d. *Sentence*: transported for 7 years.

1852

James Gilbert, labourer. Guilty of assaulting Robert Beard Mallows and robbing him of 1s. *Sentence*: transported for 7 years.

Unbelievably, I am not making those cases up: Stock Criswell really was transported for stealing clothes off a washing-line and 'about half a pound of cheese'. Lewis Flint *was* transported for stealing goods and money to the value of 2s. 11d. James Gilbert *was* transported for stealing 1s. – and all the others are true as well. The only one I could not believe was the case of Samuel Gilbert and John Baines, until I actually held the 'true bill' in my own hands. I can assure you that they really were transported for seven years apiece for stealing 'one live tame duck'.

But what did transportation actually mean for these Gamlingay people? Transporting convicts to penal settlements had been practised since the seventeenth century, usually (after its discovery) to Australia – originally to Botany Bay, but after the 1820s to Van Dieman's Land (Tasmania). As a method of dealing with 'criminals' transportation left a lot to be desired, and between 1853 and 1864 the idea was gradually phased out. For people like Elizabeth Bartle, those three members of the Gilbert family, Lewis Flint and the rest it meant serving a period in the terrible 'hulks' – floating, rotten prison ships – before being put on a ship to Australia. Once on board the convict ship the prisoners were bound in chains for the journey to the other side of the world. Thousands of people perished on the voyage. Assuming they survived, the convicts then served out their sentences on various estates throughout Australia, poorly fed and badly treated.

When the convict had served his sentence, there he usually remained, unable to buy a return passage for several years, if ever. In other words, transportation meant being torn from one's family with little hope of ever seeing them again, to become a slave-labourer in Australia. So far as I can discover, none of the people from Gamlingay ever returned to their homes.

No wonder the labourers were bitter.

31

The Final Act

The period from 1830 until 1850 is the low point in the fortunes of the labourers and, by extension, of the village itself. We have seen how the bond-peasant of the Middle Ages was in many ways more free and independent than the cowed and brutalised labourers of the 1840s. At least the medieval peasant had his common rights, the right to graze animals at certain times on the village land, the right to gather fuel from certain places at certain times, and so forth. The labourer of the 1840s had in most villages lost even these rights, although it took until the end of the decade for labourers in Gamlingay to lose theirs.

The reason the labourers lost their rights is very simple. Even the dimmest and most ill-educated villager must have known that the end of commons, open fields and the ancient way of agriculture was in sight. Enclosure had been going on piecemeal for centuries, resulting in there being by the 1830s almost as much enclosed land in the parish as there was unenclosed arable. Over 1,800 acres was still held as it always had been, in individual strips, and was farmed in the three-field rotation way as it always had been. Most of the rest of East Anglia and the Midlands had already been enclosed in the second half of the eighteenth century and the early part of the nineteenth. The trouble with Gamlingay was that it lacked the controlling hand of a resident squire, able to take on the costs of enclosure: securing an Act of Parliament, buying mile upon mile of fencing, and so on. The idea had been mooted many times as the answer to the village's problems, not least by Alfred Power, who said: 'inclosure . . . would give them great temporary relief, and better them permanently to a certain degree' ('them' being the impoverished farmers, and not the labourers). But there were always objections, from the poor, who would lose their common rights, from Merton College and from others who objected to the expense of enclosure, and because of the 'difficulty of arranging satisfactorily to all parties with respect to the tithes'.

Following an Act of Parliament in 1836 it became possible to save a large part of the expense connected with enclosure. The need for a private Act was dispensed with, and enclosure by consent was allowed, as long as two-thirds of the 'interested parties' agreed. The largest land-owner, Merton College, after dragging its heels for nearly a century, changed its mind, and the destruction of the ancient village that is the theme of this book could begin.

Commissioners were appointed to parcel out new fields in proportion to the ownership of strips in the common fields. Surveyors measured the whole parish accurately and produced a new map in 1844, drawing large fields with straight boundaries in typically rigid Victorian style to replace the old higgledy-piggledy medieval furlongs and strips. A new road (still called 'New Road') was made, linking the Cambridge and Hatley roads for the first time. Those people, some seventy or so, with common rights and perhaps a strip or two in the open fields were granted smallholdings or allotments in compensation.

The commons were common no more, save for six acres renamed 'Recreation Ground' and preserved as common ground on the northern edge of the parish. Public roads were clearly defined and given regular verges. Those ancient trackways and strips of pasture known as hadens, deans, ways and slades which ran between the furlongs were either incorporated in the new fields or became 'Private Carriage Roads and Driftways' allotted to the appropriate landholders. Fourteen footpaths became 'discontinued rights of way'. Instead of being able to wander at will over practically the entire parish, villagers were restricted to public rights of way and their own property. Soon they would be confronted with notices painted with the words 'trespassers will be prosecuted' – a legal nonsense, but

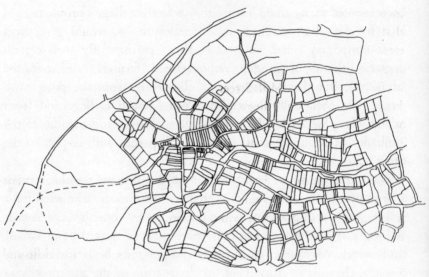

Sketch map of furlongs in 1602

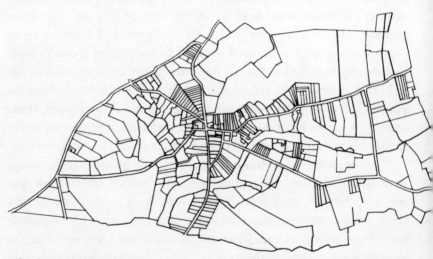

Sketch map of fields in 1850

These two maps give a vivid idea of the results of enclosure. The ancient open fie parish was a patchwork of irregular furlongs, each with its own descriptive nam After the Victorian Enclosure Commissioners had imposed their rigid geometry the landscape only the old enclosures around the village core remained indicative of the new order of things. It was an enormous upheaval in the landscape, and a millenium of history was swept away virtually overnight.

As an example of the effects of enclosure on a single farm, let us look at Blythe Farm, in Mill Street. Blythe Farm was owned by Clare Hall, a Cambridge College, and in 1794 consisted of 111 acres, of which 98 were arable, the rest made up of the farmhouse and farm buildings, and 11 acres of pasture in Cow Lane Close. The main 98-acre holding in the open fields was surveyed in 1794, when it was known as 'Apthorpe Farm'. By chance, the map that was made following the survey has survived in private hands. It shows that those holdings were split almost equally among the three great common fields: 33 in Shortwood Field, 30 in Middle Field, and 35 in Potton Wood Field (the names correspond to the medieval East, Middle and South fields respectively). These holdings were subdivided into strips, the 98 acres being made up of more than *130* separate strips, consisting on average of one or two ridges, and scattered the length and breadth of the parish. It must have been terribly difficult to farm them properly.

Following the Enclosure Award fifty years later those 130–odd strips were taken from Clare and in return they were given one huge field of their own. The same procedure was followed throughout the parish, landholding by landholding, until the new village was laid out to the satisfaction of all the interested parties, and the Enclosure Award finally confirmed in 1848.

The result was a landscape of large, regular fields, each in single ownership, enabling enterprising farmers to put into practice new, intensive farming methods. They could drain their lands, fertilise them, and grow precisely the crops they wanted to grow without having to consult or consider their neighbours. It also enabled one or two farmers to build outlying farms away from the main village, in the middle of their own land. With another 700 acres of 'waste' land available for use as arable, it enabled the wealthier landowners to become even more prosperous and grow even further apart from the rest of the village.

In the long run the village benefited from enclosure. It became recognisably modern in aspect and in its farming methods. But what of the poor labourers, robbed even of their common rights? Much has been written on this subject by historians, and the effects of enclosure exaggerated by some. The right to graze a cow or two on the commons was all very well, but you had to own one before you could take advantage of that right. Few labourers could afford to buy more than the bare necessities to sustain themselves, let alone buy and maintain a cow. Losing the right to gather fuel was, no doubt, a serious blow for some and probably made them worse off than before, until the railways arrived and relatively cheap coal became available. The most important result of enclosure for the labourers was that without common rights they became totally dependent on the wages they could earn, and even more at the mercy of the farmers.

The final act of demolition of the old village came a couple of years later when the much-resented system of paying tithes in kind to the church was commuted for a fixed payment instead.

Gamlingay had finally and irrevocably changed. Since 1279 (and long before) men and women had worked the land in partnership in order to survive. They used the traditional three-field rotation system, held their land in strips all over the parish, co-operating with each other, sometimes reluctantly, because they had to. They lived for the most part within the village itself. They were a distinct community. Slowly, though, economic and social forces had changed the villagers from medieval peasants and bondmen into farmers and landless labourers, the open fields to regular, privately-owned ones, the village from one community into two. Now there were, on the one hand, those stalwarts of the Victorian parish recorded in county directories – the gentry, landowners, farmers, publicans and tradesmen; and there were, on the other hand, those people ignored by the directories whose lives were spent in grudging silence before their betters. In other words, by 1850 there is in operation the fully developed, typically English, class system.

Conclusion

The year 1850 marks the end of this story but by no means the end of Gamlingay's story. History is a story without end.

I spoke of the Gamlingay of 1850 containing two villages: the dark, unplumbable one of poverty and despair, and the other, the 'directory' village of farmers, landowners and tradesmen. As much of the last few chapters was taken up with the poor, let us look at the other side of the village, as seen through the eyes of one of those directories: Gardner's *History, Gazetteer & Directory* of Cambridgeshire, published in 1851.

Eight of the inhabitants listed are noted separately and are obviously of superior caste to the rest: Sir Williamson Booth; the Reverend Doctor James, rector; George Heckford, surgeon; William Hepworth; Enoch Manning, the Baptist minister; Mrs Ann Paine; James Paine, esquire of Brook End House, and William Wilkieson. Booth and Wilkieson 'reside at Woodbury'. Then come the farmers – eleven of these – Dews, Paines, Tophams, Woodhams, etc. – followed by the traders. Six licensed victuallers are listed, at the Bull, Falcon, Chequers, Cock, Oak and Wheatsheaf, whose establishments were used by what it is now permissible to call the middle classes. At a lower level come the nine 'beer retailers', whose humble and unnamed beerhouses had been licensed for the first time in 1830. They were used by labourers and others of the lower orders. Other trades mentioned in the Directory include two blacksmiths, three builders, two saddlers, two grocers and drapers, a carpenter, two bakers, a butcher, a tailor, a milliner, wheelwright, shoemaker, ironmonger and a 'carrier to Cambridge'. All are typically rural occupations and such people could have been found in the village at virtually any time from the Middle Ages to World War 2.

The population was rising rapidly. In 1801 the first census recorded 847 inhabitants; in 1831 there were 1319; and by 1851 the number had risen to almost 1900, more than double the figure at the turn of the century. Yet Gardner lists only fifty-six people. Fifty-six names out of 1900 shows what a large proportion of the village belonged to that other, twilight world. What of them? Some were servants, employed in the houses of those at or near the top of the tree. Some were children; some were old; some were housewives tied to large families. Most of the men and boys worked on the land.

Agriculture was the largest employer of labour in the village, with much extra work being necessary following enclosure: fencing, ditching, draining and so on. Farming was heavily labour-intensive. A lot of labour was needed to carry on the progressive farming methods which replaced open-field agriculture. Farming, in fact, went through something of a golden age during the 1850s, '60s and early '70s, when prices were buoyant and the boom in urban development provided a ready and expanding market.

Sending produce to these new outlets became much easier after 1862, when the railway eventually arrived. Part of the Oxford-Bedford-Cambridge route, the line was built in a long, gentle curve from Potton through the south-eastern corner of the parish. It followed the course of the brook, and some small embankments and cuttings were necessary before the line left the parish and headed for Cambridge. The station was built a mile or so away from the village, which meant a long walk for people who wished to use the new facility. Not that many ordinary folk could afford the fares, which only came within reach of the majority of people later in the century. To some villagers the railway meant work; not well-paid work, but work nonetheless, and relatively secure. Theoretically it brought Gamlingay in particular, and rural England in general, into much closer contact with the rest of the world. Locally I suspect that most of its real impact was on farmers, and that it did not make much difference to anyone else. The railway, like the new regular fields it sliced through, quickly became an accepted part of the village landscape.

Two other areas of employment opened up in the decades following enclosure. One was in the mining of coprolites (nodules of phosphate of calcium) which when treated produced an artifical fertiliser of great value to progressive farmers. Coprolites were mined during the 1860s in a mad scramble of coprolite fever as landowners sought to exploit the new-found wealth beneath the soil, and labourers found lucrative employment in digging it out. There were no coprolites in Gamlingay, but plenty in the Potton and Sandy area. In 1867 the rector pointed out to a Royal commission that the 'coprolite diggings in our neighbourhood have occupied very many of our boys, many of whom earn at them 8s. and 9s. a week, which is more than the farmers can give them'. It was very nearly as much as the farmers gave their men.

The other, and longer-term, area of new employment was in brickmaking. Bricks had probably always been made in the village, but most of the best brick-earth was to be found under the Heath, on common land. After enclosure the Heath became available for exploitation, and it was exploited for all it was worth. One of the two brickworks established on the Heath was a smallish set-up which continued production into this century, but it paled into insignificance in comparison with 'Bellevue Brickworks'. By 1912 Bellevue Brickworks had gobbled up thirty-one acres of land in one enormous pit, surrounded by the attendant plant: kilns of various sorts and sheds with a capacity of half a million bricks. The works produced tiles and pipes as well as sewer bricks, fancy bricks and the rusty-red facing bricks that went into most of the village houses that were built during this period. For sixty years the brickworks provided an alternative to the tyranny of the land, but by 1922 the works were closed, the specially-built railway sidings fell into disuse and the pit was allowed to fill with water.

Farming remained the main source of work, although after enclosure the way the land was used altered appreciably. Arable farming continued in the new fields much as before, with wheat, barley and oats as the main crops, particularly on the heavy clay. On the lighter soils many people began to use their allotments as market gardens. By 1896 fourteen men were earning their living in this way, and some small farmers had split their fields into half-acre strips and were growing market garden crops. Labourers' wages were still low.

Worse than low wages was the terrible condition of the cottages that so many of the labourers were forced to live in. As with the administration of the Poor Law earlier in the century, Gamlingay's cottages were described as being some of the worst in Cambridgeshire. In 1865 Dr Hunter, the Privy Council's Medical Officer, reported that Gamlingay

contains some of the most miserable cots met with anywhere. Some of Mr Woollam's are more execrable than any group in the county. They are in advanced stages of dilapidation . . .

the poorest thatched hovel is sure of a tenant, for it is part of the straw plait country . . .

a deadly lassitude, a hopeless surrendering up to filth, affects Gamlingay, and the neglect of the centre becomes mortification at the extremities, north and south, where the houses are rotting to pieces . . .

£3 is a common rent for a wretched hut, and one not worth £20 was let at £2 15s. Eight and nine people were found in the single bedroomed houses, and in two cases six adults slept in a room with a child or two.

Comment is superfluous, except with regard to straw-plaiting. This was a true cottage industry, especially in Bedfordshire, where Luton was the centre of the straw-hat trade. Thousands of village womenfolk and children were employed at home plaiting straw. The plait, in many different patterns, was sold to people who stitched them into bags, hats, bonnets and baskets. Making pillow-lace, too, was an important women's occupation. It was produced on a three-legged frame called a pillow-horse. Many women and young girls ruined their eyesight and damaged their spines working at a pillow-horse. By the turn of the century pillow-lace and straw-plaiting had declined, and only one or two older women still practised the arts. Changing fashions and the introduction of new machinery killed off these rural industries. I have a photograph of Susannah Panter, taken early this century, which shows her sitting at her pillow-horse on the path outside her house. She wears glasses and sits in a slightly hunched position, an old woman (born a mere ten years after the Battle of Waterloo), photographed as a curiosity in Edwardian England.

Where children worked, as most of them did, their formal education was frequently neglected. The 1870 Education Act set up non-denominational, secular elementary schools managed by school boards, and in 1880 school attendance was made compulsory up to the age of ten. Before these Acts there were only the two schools built in 1848 by the Baptists and the Church of England available to village children, and few poor families could see any benefit from spending precious pennies on educating their children. Neither the National School nor the British School survived the establishment of the Board School in 1874 – a large, ugly Victorian building which still provides village children with their primary education.

Poverty became more acute following the agricultural depression of the 1870s. It became cheaper to grow wheat on the vast American prairies and ship it to England than to grow it in places like Gamlingay and send it to market by horse and cart or train. Many farmers, especially the smaller ones, gave up the unequal struggle and sold out.

In 1887 another parliamentary enquiry into the state of agriculture found that in this corner of Cambridgeshire the effects of the depression were to make considerable tracts of land virtually worthless. Even someone as well-off as Octavius Wedd, who lived in Fowlmere, near Cambridge, but who had a farm in Gamlingay, was hard up and anxious for money, as two letters to John Dew (still kept by the Dew family) illustrate. On 24 November 1886 Octavious Wedd wrote to John Dew, 'Go to St Neots with the Barley & do the best you can with it, if you don't see me on Thursday, *only sell it*'. (My italics.) Four days later he wrote, 'By this mornings Post I heard about my Barley at Cambridge Market yesterday and the Trade was awful. There was no selling ordinary Barley into money; with all the buyers in that great Market perhaps one would make a bid of 4 or 5/– under what he was asked. I wish you would go over to your Uncles at Caxton before he goes to St Ives and ask him to take it there and *turn it into money somehow*'. (Wedd's italics.)

With farmers in such straights labourers could not demand higher wages. Children's earnings, little though they were for such tasks as bird-scaring or light labouring, were nonetheless a valuable source of income. Many of the children, especially girls, were destined to become servants in the houses of the wealthy.

The reality of Gamlingay in the period from the start of the agricultural depression until World War 1 was poverty – poor farms, poor farmers and even poorer labourers. The general picture did not change much until World War 1 had mangled many younger men in the trenches, and even then farming continued to be depressed well into the 1930s. My father and others of his generation, the sons and daughters of farm labourers, who were growing up in the years before the outbreak of World War 2, can still recall the poverty and the pangs of hunger. The village stagnated during those inter-war years. Despite the crying need for better housing, little building work was done, although a few council houses were built for those who could afford the rent.

World War 2 marked the end of an era. The village changed more quickly in the forty-odd post-war years than it ever had in the previous millennium. Farming was being concentrated into fewer and fewer hands. Other areas of employment opened up and farmworkers left the land in droves. Market gardening, once so important both as a full-time occupation for some and a part-time one for farm labourers, has gradually declined until only a few people work as market gardeners today.

It is the revolution in agriculture, however, largely unnoticed outside rural villages, that has wrought the greatest change. In 1871 William Paine farmed 430 acres in Gamlingay, and employed fifteen men and eight boys, with extra help brought in at harvest. Carting, ploughing, barrowing and so forth was done slowly and laboriously by men and horses, while dozens of jobs such as lifting potatoes or parsnips, or weeding, were all done manually. Small armies of men armed with scythes and sickles would enter a field at harvest and physically cut every ear of corn by hand. There had been some technical innovation, like the introduction of steam ploughing and reaper-binders, but by and large the sweat of men and animals oiled the wheels of agriculture. Large numbers of craftsmen (wheelwrights, blacksmiths, saddlers and so on) relied on farmers for their living.

Tractors heralded the coming revolution, arriving slowly during the 1920s and '30s. Within a decade or two after World War I the lure of higher wages and the introduction of machinery had drastically cut farm labour-forces. The situation has now altered so much that whereas a century ago William Paine needed fifteen men and eight boys on his 430 acres all year round, and many others beside at harvest, the present farmer of Merton's land – some 600 acres – needs only two men to crop and harvest it. Moreover, they produce yields beyond the wildest dreams of men like William Paine. Forty years ago a farmer would have been well satisfied with a yield of a ton of wheat per acre. Now he is not satisfied with a yield of two and a half tons per acre. Gangs of toiling men wielding scythes have been replaced by the driver of an enormous, highly efficient combine harvester. Sitting in his soundproofed, air-conditioned cab he harvests more wheat in a day than a dozen men could have cut by hand in a week. Fifty years ago a horse and man could plough an acre a day. A tractor will plough twenty-five acres and more in a day, and any weeds that dare raise their heads are destroyed by chemicals as soon as they appear. Virtually any task once undertaken by men and women can be done more quickly and efficiently by machine. It is the biggest revolution that the countryside has ever seen.

There is now a new Gamlingay, very different from that of even fifty years ago. During the 1960s there was an increase in building both by the Council and by private firms, resulting in a large influx of outsiders, mainly from the London area. The population has increased. From its peak in 1871 when it topped 2,000, the population fell with the agricultural depression and the closure of the brickworks to a low of just over 1,400 in 1931. Thirty years later in 1961 there were still only 1,551 people living in the village. So rapid has been the increase since then that at the last census in 1981 there were slightly over 3,200 living in Gamlingay. In twenty years the population more than doubled, and with that growth there has been a corresponding increase in amenities. Village shops have increased in number. There are playgroups, various societies, evening classes of all descriptions, a new community centre, and leisure facilities of all kinds, many of them run by newcomers. Education is catered for by the infant's school (the old board school) and a village college, built in 1965, that acts as a middle school. For education beyond the age of thirteen village children travel by bus to an upper school. Many people now work outside the village, and some commute to London.

Other physical changes have occurred, not all of them for the better. During the building boom of the 1960s and early '70s the village lost two priceless houses, both at the crossroads – Whitehall, built in the late sixteenth-century, and Cross Farm, a rambling seventeenth-century farmhouse – as well as several lesser old and interesting buildings. Acre upon acre of farmland has been covered with a sprawl of housing estates, none of them architecturally different from those to be found in any town or village in England. Every spare inch of land is slowly being covered with bricks and mortar. Footpaths have been ploughed up, and even Avenel's moat is no more, the last surviving arm filled in to provide a few more square yards of wheat for the farmer.

The railway station was closed in the late 1960s and the railway line ripped up. Soon after, a small industrial estate appeared beside the now redundant station, providing more employment in the village. There is even a commercial vineyard in the parish. But the village has ceased to be an agricultural community and has become a part of commuterland. I was born in a Gamlingay that was still very much a village in the early 1950s. My son is growing up in what is virtually a small town in the 1980s, with no real identity of its own as yet. Modern planners cannot take all the blame, and, I am happy to report, were responsible for the correction of one historical anomaly: in 1965 Woodbury, tacked on to the parish for the sake of ecclesiastical convenience in the dim and distant past, but never really *of* it, was at last transferred to Bedfordshire, where it belongs.

As the modern village grows there has been a corresponding awareness of the historical value of the older buildings which still survive. Several, notably the old rectory (now called 'The Emplins') and Merton Manor Farm, have been lovingly restored to a glory they have never known before in their long histories. Life seldom consists of black and white choices, but there can be little doubt that if you weigh things up, then present-day villagers enjoy a cleaner, healthier, higher standard of living than their fathers and grandfathers would ever have thought possible. There is an environmental price for all this progress, of course. How we choose to pay it is for the future to decide.

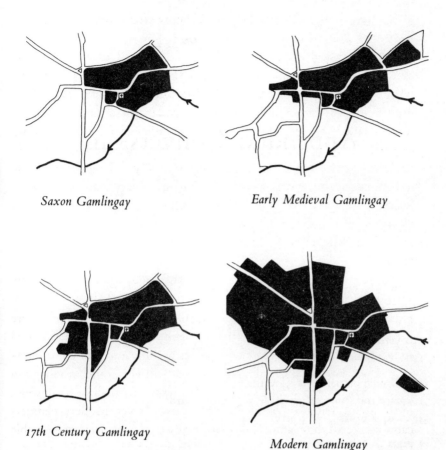

Saxon Gamlingay

Early Medieval Gamlingay

17th Century Gamlingay

Modern Gamlingay

These maps illustrate the ebb and flow of Gamlingay over the centuries. The Saxon village was laid out east to west along the Bedford–Cambridge road, with good access to the brook and the green. During the early medieval period there was a growth in population and the village expanded both east and west. Not shown is the outlying hamlet of Newton, which grew up to the west of the village and was then abandoned around 1230. After the Black Death the village shrank considerably. By the seventeenth century the focus of the village had shifted towards the crossroads. This was almost certainly due to the growth of St Ives in the Middle Ages and the consequent importance of the north–south Biggleswade to St Ives road. Modern Gamlingay has grown enormously in the post-1960s housing boom. What the map does not show is the way almost every square yard of what was once field, garden or backyard within the village core has been filled with houses.

Appendix: Conversions

1 inch = 2.54 centimetres
12 inches = 1 foot
3 feet = 1 yard
220 yards = 1 furlong
1760 yards = 1 mile

1 rod, pole or perch = $5\frac{1}{2}$ yards
1 square rod, pole or perch = $30\frac{1}{4}$ square yards
4840 square yards = 1 acre

2 pints = 1 quart
4 quarts = 1 gallon
2 gallons = 1 peck
4 pecks = 1 bushel
4 bushels = 1 coomb
2 coombs = 1 quarter

12 pennies (12d.) = 1 shilling (1s.)
20 shillings = 1 pound (£1)
21 shillings = 1 guinea
240 pennies in 1 pound
1 new penny = 2.4 old ones

I cannot give any equivalents between prices and money in the past and today. The period covered is too long, and prices always depend on whether one is buying or selling. Besides, money was not as important in the Middle Ages as it is today, for instance, when payment was frequently made in kind. Even if you iron out those difficulties, like is still not being compared to like. How can you compare the wages of a thatcher in 1300, when they were ubiquitous, and a thatcher today, who has little competition and is continually in demand? Or the price of a horse in 1580 with that of a horse in 1980? One is a working animal, the other a luxury item. Such comparisons are meaningless.

Select Bibliography

These are some of the books I used in one way or another while researching this one.

GENERAL

Bennett, H.S., *Life on the English Manor* (Cambridge University Press, Cambridge, 1937).

Emmison, F.G., The *Elizabethan Life* series published by Essex County Council: *Home, Work and Land* (Chelmsford, 1976); *Disorder* (Chelmsford, 1970); *Morals and the Church Courts* (Chelmsford 1973).

Gooder, E.A., *Latin for Local History* (Longman, London, 1961).

Harrison, J.F.C., *The Common People* (Fontana, London, 1984).

Harvey, P.D.A., (ed), *Manorial Records of Cuxham, Oxfordshire c1200–1359* (HMSO, London, 1976).

Hoskins, W.G., *Local History in England* (Longman, London, 1959).

Laslett, P., *The World We Have Lost* (Methuen, London, 1965).

Latham, R.E., *Revised Medieval Latin Word-List* (British Academy, London, 1965).

Mingay, G.E., *Rural Life in Victorian England* (Heinemann, London, 1977).

Richardson, J., *The Local Historian's Encyclopedia* (Historical Publications, London, 1974).

Tate, W.E., *The Parish Chest* (Cambridge University Press, Cambridge, 1946).

West, J., *Village Records* (Macmillan, London, 1962).

Ziegler, P., *The Black Death* (Collins, London, 1969).

LOCAL:

Carter, E., *History of the County of Cambridge* (Cambridge, 1753).

Conybeare, J.W.E., *History of Cambridgeshire* (London, 1897).

Gibbons, A., *Ely Episcopal Records* (Lincoln, 1891).

Gooch, W., *General View of the Agriculture of the County of Cambridge* (Board of Agriculture, London, 1813).

Palmer, W.M., *The Assize held at Cambridge, A.D. 1260* (Linton, 1930).

Documents relating to the Cambridgeshire Villages (with H. Saunders, Cambridge, no date).

Episcopal Visitation Returns for Cambridgeshire, 1638–65 (Cambridge, 1930).

Parker, R., *The Common Stream* (Collins, London, 1975).

Cottage on the Green (Parker, Foxton, 1973).

On the Road – The Papworth Story (Pendragon Press, Cambridge, 1977).

Royal Commission on Historical Monuments, England, *West Cambridgeshire* (HMSO, London, 1968).

Vancouver, C., *General View of the Agriculture in the County of Cambridge* (Board of Agriculture, London, 1794).

Victoria County History, *Cambridgeshire and the Isle of Ely* (HMSO).

MAIN DOCUMENTARY SOURCES

Bodleian Library, Oxford

Thomas Langdon's 1602 maps of the Merton Estates

Cambridge County Record Office

Printed:
Rotuli Hundredorum.
Vetus Liber Archidiaconi Eliensis.

Microfilm:
Cole Manuscripts.

Manuscripts:
Quarter Session Order Books.

Churchwardens' Accounts.
Overseers' Accounts.
Constables' Accounts.
Apprenticeship Bonds and Indentures.
Parish Registers.
Enclosure Award and Map.

Cambridgeshire Collection, Cambridge Central Library

Cambridge Chronicle Files.

Gamlingay Baptish Church

Church Minute Book.

Merton College, Oxford

Manor Court Rolls.
Bailiff Accounts.
Rentals and Surveys.

Public Record Office

Star Chamber Records.
Prerogative Court of Canterbury Wills.

University Library, Cambridge

Printed:
Poor Law Commissioners' Reports.

Manuscripts:
Archdeacon's Visitation Records.
Archdeaconry Wills.
Woodbury Rental 1672.

In Private Hands

Estate Map of Clare Farm.
Octavius Wedd's letters.

Index